HOLDING FORTH THE
Word of Life

Walter P. Brown

Walt Brown
Proverbs 3:5-6

PAGE PUBLISHING, INC.
New York, NY

First originally published by Page Publishing, Inc. 2017

ISBN 978-1-63568-176-5 (Paperback)
ISBN 978-1-63568-177-2 (Digital)

The Scriptures are from the King James Bible with and occasional
quote from the New King James.

Printed in the United States of America

Preface

The compilation of this work would not have been possible without the assistance of my precious wife, Kathy, the love of my life for over sixty years. She edited each devotion, corrected my grammatical errors, and then typed each one distributed weekly by e-mail. Words are totally inadequate to express my love and appreciation for her.

Together, we dedicate this labor of love to our wonderful Lord and Savior, Jesus Christ, for the continuance of the Gospel and the building up in the faith of his children. We pray he will use each devotion, which was written prayerfully under the leadership of his Holy Spirit, to the honor and glory of his holy name!

In His Love,

Walter P. Brown

Isaiah 55:11 "So shall My word be that goes forth from My mouth; It shall not return to Me void, but it shall accomplish what I please. And it shall prosper in the thing for which I send it."

The Word of God

Isaiah 48:17 "Thus saith the Lord thy Redeemer, the Holy One of Israel: I am the Lord thy God, who teacheth thee to profit, who leadeth thee by the way that thou shouldest go."

Our minds can hardly begin to comprehend the magnitude of our Triune God; Father, Son, and Holy Spirit. In Jesus's day, society was very divided as to whether or not he was the Christ. John 7:43 "So there was a division among the people because of Him." Some said, "Of a truth this is the Prophet" (John 7:40b). While others said "This is the Christ" (John 7:41a). The skeptics said, "Shall Christ come out of Galilee?" (John 7:41b). It is interesting to me that as the chief priest and Pharisees send officers to take Jesus, they came back without him and said "never man spoke like this man" (John 7:46b). Truer words were never spoken, for this man was God incarnate, the Word made flesh!

My mind turns to a beautiful song that we never hear anymore, "There's Something That's Different About Him." While I cannot recall all the words, I do remember one verse says, "His voice can calm the angry sea, and although I can't explain, my life is different since He came. There's something that's different about Him." He is indeed our Redeemer, the Holy One, the Alpha and Omega, the Beginning and the End.

One thing about society has not changed since the day Jesus walked this earth. Men are still very much divided about who he is. Some say he is a prophet or a teacher, perhaps a good man. However, to those of us who know him as Savior and Lord, we say with Peter, "Thou art the Christ, the Son of the living God." As we think of a world of lost and dying men, our hearts cry out with the psalmist, "Oh that men would praise the Lord for His goodness and for His wonderful works to the children of men" (Psalm 107:8).

It is my firm belief that we are ever so near to our Lord's second coming and then for many, it will be too late to repent of sin and trust him as Savior and Lord. Revelation 19: 11–16 "And I saw heaven opened and behold, a white horse; and he that sat upon him was called Faithful and True, and in righteousness he does judge and make war. His eyes were like a flame of fire and on his head were many crowns; and he had a name written that no man knew but he himself. And he was clothed with a vesture dipped in blood; and his name is called The Word of God. And the armies that were in heaven followed him upon white horses, clothed in fine linen, white and clean. And out of his mouth goeth a sharp sword that with it he should smite the nations, and he shall rule them with a rod of iron; and he treadeth the winepress of the fierceness and wrath of Almighty God. And he has on his vesture and on his thigh a name written, King of Kings and Lord of Lords."

The Written Word

Second Timothy 3:16–17 "All Scripture is given by inspiration of God and is profitable for doctrine, for reproof, for correction, for instruction in righteousness, that the man of God may be perfect. thoroughly furnished unto all good works."

In his love and by his grace, the Living Word spoke his Word to holy men of God, who spoke as they were moved by the Holy Spirit to provide for us the written Word of God. How blessed we are indeed to have in our possession a copy of God's Holy Word, amazingly composed, divinely inspired, and miraculously preserved throughout the history of mankind. There are people groups in this world who would give anything to own a copy of God's Word in their native language; yet we as Christians here in America take it for granted. It may be the best-selling book in our country, but I wonder if it is the best read!

Consider the words of Paul as he writes to Timothy, and to us, concerning scripture. He clearly defines its origin—the divinely inspired Word from God himself. That very thought, it seems, would cause every believer to want to take time every single day to spend alone with the Heavenly Father, asking him to speak specifically to our hearts from his Word.

The scripture is our source for life and living. From the cradle to the grave, it can guide us in our walk with the Lord. It begins with salvation. "From a child thou has known the Holy Scriptures, which are able to make you wise unto salvation through faith which is in Christ Jesus" (2 Timothy 3:15). It is from hearing or reading the scripture that we first learn the Gospel story, which brings us to repentance of sin and faith in the finished work of Christ, all under the leading of God's Holy Spirit. The Bible says, "Faith cometh by hearing and hearing by the Word of God" (Romans 10:17). It is essential, after salvation, to spend time in God's Word in order to grow in grace and knowledge. The ultimate objective is to be a perfect (mature) man of God, ready always to give an answer for the hope that is within us. Note: Our text outlines four important objectives for our lives found in scripture. It is profitable for doctrine, for reproof, for correction, and for instruction in righteousness.

Doctrine: How crucial it is to know and believe sound doctrine. Many today are teaching and preaching false doctrine. In some circles, the Gospel is so watered down it is beyond recognition. The Bible clearly addresses the issue of false doctrine and alerts us to be on guard. "I marvel that you are so soon removed from Him that called you into the grace of Christ unto another gospel, which is not another; but there are some that trouble you and would pervert the Gospel of Christ. But though we, or an angel from heaven, preach another gospel unto you than which we have preached unto you, let him be accursed" (Galatians 1:6–8).

Another note of warning comes to us from John the Beloved, who writes, "Beloved, believe not every spirit, but test the spirits whether they are of God; because many false prophets are gone out into the world" (1 John 4:1). The only way you and I can recognize truth and sound doctrine is by prayerfully studying God's Word.

The Written Word

Second Timothy 2:15 "Study to show thyself approved unto God, a workman that needeth not to be ashamed, rightly dividing the word of truth."

Doctrine

We learned from our text in 2 Timothy 3:16–17 that scripture is profitable for doctrine, for reproof, for correction, for instruction in righteousness. While I have no desire to engage in a confrontation with other denominations regarding their doctrinal beliefs, it is most important for believers to be well grounded in scripture and sound doctrine. It is my very firm belief that as we move closer to the return of our Lord, we will see more and more of a falling away from the truth. We are encouraged "that we henceforth be no more children, tossed to and fro and carried about with every wind of doctrine, by the sleight [trickery] of men, and cunning craftiness by which they lie in wait to deceive" (Ephesians 4:14). False doctrine is abundant in our society, even among many Baptists. For instance, consider the recent New Baptist Covenant Celebration in Atlanta.

Upon reading some of the comments made at this gathering, it is no wonder the SBC and New Baptist Covenant parted company. I share some of the following information, not to cast a snare on anyone, but so you may be aware of what is happening and to see how the Gospel is being incorrectly interpreted, taught, and preached by some. Novelist John Grisham had this to say, and I quote: "In the Baptist Church of my youth, we were taught that the Bible is the infallible, inerrant Word of God ... every word is divinely inspired and it is to be read literally. It just dropped out of Heaven. The Church was proudly intolerant of other people, other denominations; other religions." End quote. You can see where Mr. Grisham is going with this. Another pastor, Gerald Durley, went even further by denying the divine inspiration of scripture and totally misrepresenting truth. I quote his comments from the Louisiana 330 News, "Baptists need to get over the desire to convert everyone to faith in Christ and appreciate the beauty of religions like Islam." He went on to say, "John 14:6 does not necessarily mean that Jesus is the only way to salvation and compared the religions of the world to a vegetable soup that is flavorful because of its diversity." End quote. Unbelievable! I would not want to be in that pastor's shoes at the judgment seat of Christ.

Does doctrine really matter? Let me quote John MacArthur. "God holds us accountable for what we believe as well as how we think about the truth He has revealed. All Scripture testifies to the fact that God wants us to know and understand the truth. He wants us to be wise. His will is that we use our minds. We are supposed to think, meditate and above all, to be discerning. The content of our faith is crucial. Sincerity is not enough." End quote. As Pastor J. Paul Driscoll used to say, "We can be sincere, but sincerely wrong."

Let me close with a strong word from 1 Timothy 6:3–5 "If any man teach otherwise and consent not to wholesome words, even the words of our Lord Jesus Christ and to the doctrine which is according to godliness, he is proud, knowing nothing, but doting about questions and disputes of words, of which come envy, strife, railings, evil suspicions, perverse disputings of men of corrupt minds and destitute of the truth, supposing that gain is godliness; from such withdraw thyself."

The Written Word (continued)

> First Timothy 4:16 "Take heed unto thyself and unto the doctrine; continue in them; for in doing this thou shalt both save thyself and them that hear thee."

Sound doctrine was the mark of the early Church. "They continued steadfastly in the apostles' doctrine and fellowship and in breaking of bread and in prayers" (Acts 2:42). This was the testimony of believers after Pentecost and facilitated by the moving of God's Holy Spirit; and it was the reason the Church grew in numbers and in spirit. It is apparent, even in this twenty-first century that, in spite of the wickedness of our society, a church that preaches and teaches unashamedly, the Gospel of our Lord Jesus Christ with sound doctrine, will flourish and grow a strong body of believers. The opposite is also true. The reason so many churches in America are dead and lifeless is because they are more concerned with what is politically correct than they are with being devoted to sound doctrine and the preaching and teaching of the Gospel.

It was Apostle Paul who said, "For I am not ashamed of the Gospel of Christ; for it is the power of God unto salvation to everyone that believeth; to the Jew first and also to the Greek. For in it is the righteousness of God revealed from faith to faith; as it is written, the just shall live by faith" (Romans 1:16–17). The Gospel is the power (dynamite) of God that alone can transform the lives of men! Then, in writing to young Timothy, Paul writes, "Till I come, give attendance to reading, to exhortation, to doctrine" (1 Timothy 4:13).

Let us summarize some of the truths and words of encouragement to us from these few passages today. First, a word of caution in that we are "to take heed unto ourselves and unto the doctrine." To me, this means that I study truthful and accurate doctrine and apply it first and foremost to my own life. In doing this continually, our walk with the Lord will be pleasing to him and our testimony of his grace and love will have an impact on others with whom we share and pray for. It was Oswald Chambers who said, "You can never give another person that which you have found, but you can make him homesick for what you have."

We are also encouraged, like the early believers, to continue steadfastly in the apostle's doctrine, in fellowship, and in prayer. It is crucial, especially in these last days, to assemble with believers of like faith and doctrine. "Not forsaking the assembling of ourselves together, as the manner of some is, but exhorting one another and so much more as you see the day approaching" (Hebrews 10:25). Then we are to read, to encourage one another and share sound doctrine. This happens to be one of the main objectives of the Word for the Week. We pray that each and every reader will be encouraged and challenged to spend time in God's Word.

The Living Word

Hebrews 4:12 "For the word of God is living and powerful
and sharper than any two-edged sword, piercing even to the
dividing asunder of soul and spirit and of the joints and marrow
and is a discerner of the thoughts and intents of the heart."

Our Lord Jesus Christ is the living Word. The Gospel of John defines him well. "In the beginning was the Word and the Word was with God and the Word was God. The same was in the beginning with God. All things were made by Him; and without Him was not anything made that was made. In Him was life; and the life was the light of men. And the light shineth in darkness; and the darkness overcame it not" (John 1:1–5).

The Book of Colossians elaborates further on the pre-eminent glory of Christ. "For by Him were all things created, that are in heaven and that are in the earth, visible and invisible, whether they be thrones, or dominions, or principalities or powers…all things were created by Him and for Him; and He is before all things and by Him all things consist. And He is the Head of the body, the Church; who is the beginning, the firstborn from the dead, that in all things He might have the pre-eminence. For it pleased the Father that in Him should all fullness dwell" (Colossians 1:16–19).

"I am the Alpha and Omega, the beginning and the ending, saith the Lord, who is and who was and who is to come, the Almighty. I am He that liveth and was dead; and behold, I am alive forevermore, Amen, and have the keys of Hades and of death" (Revelation 1:8, 18). May God help us one and all to focus on our living Lord in all of his glory and majesty and offer thanks to him that loved us and washed us from our sins in his own blood. When we see him in all his glory, we identify with the prophet Isaiah who said, "'Woe is me! For I am undone, because I am a man of unclean lips and I dwell in the midst of a people of unclean lips; for mine eyes have seen the King, the Lord of hosts'" (Isaiah 6:5).

To realize that this glorious omnipotent Lord could love us so much, that he would leave his throne with all his glory in heaven and come down to a lost world to go to the cross of Calvary to redeem all who would come to him in repentance of sin, is more than our finite minds can comprehend. We are so blessed to know him and be a part of the family of God. What a treasure is ours in the Pearl of great price, the Lord Jesus Christ.

The Spoken Word

Isaiah 55:11 "So shall my word be that goeth forth out of my mouth; it shall not return unto me void, but it shall accomplish that which I please and it shall prosper in the thing where to I sent it."

The spoken Word in creation

Genesis 1:3 "And God said, let there be light: and there was light." Genesis 1:6 "And God said, let there be a firmament in the midst of the waters and let it divide the waters from the waters."

Genesis 1:9 "And God said, let the waters under the Heaven be gathered together unto one place and let the dry land appear; and it was so."

Genesis 1:11 "And God said, let the earth bring forth vegetation, the herb yielding seed and the fruit tree yielding fruit after its kind, whose seed is in itself, upon the earth; and it was so."

Genesis 1:14–15 "And God said, let there be lights in the firmament of the Heaven to divide the day from the night; and let them be for signs and for seasons and for days and years; and let them be for lights in the firmament of the Heaven to give light upon the earth and it was so."

Genesis 1:20 "And God said, let the waters bring forth abundantly the moving creature that has life and fowl that may fly above the earth in the open firmament of Heaven."

Genesis 1:24 "And God said, let the earth bring forth the living creature after its kind, cattle and creeping thing and beast of the earth after its kind; and it was so."

Genesis 1:26–27 "And God said, let us make man in our image, after our likeness; and let them have dominion over the fish of the sea and over the cattle and over all the earth and every creeping thing that creepeth upon the earth. So God created man in His own image, in the image of God created He him, male and female created He them."

The power of the spoken Word (over the elements of nature)

Matthew 8:24–26 "And behold, there arose a great tempest in the sea, insomuch that the boat was covered with the waves; but He was asleep. And His disciples came to Him and awoke Him, saying, Lord, save us; we perish. And He said unto them, Why are you fearful, O you of little faith? Then He arose and rebuked the winds and the sea; and there was a great calm."

The fig tree

Matthew 21:19 "And when He saw a fig tree along the way, He came to it and found nothing on it but leaves only and said unto it, Let no fruit grow on thee henceforth forever. And presently the fig tree withered away."

As we begin each New Year with all of its possibilities and opportunities for those who seek the Lord, I pray, by simply reviewing biblical truths about the Triune God we know and serve, that we would be encouraged by focusing on him. Wherever you find yourself, please know he is able to do exceedingly abundantly above all that we ask or think, according to the power that worketh in us.

Are you in need of the Creator, creating in you a clean heart and renewing a right spirit within you? He is able! Are you being tossed upon the sea of life, fearful, anxious, and of little faith? He can calm the storm in your life regardless of what it may be and give you peace. Like the fig tree, is your life fruitless for the Lord, with nothing but leaves? He promised if we abide in him, we can bear much fruit.

What a great time to search our hearts, confess and forsake besetting sins, and make a new commitment of our hearts and lives to him. May the Lord give each of us grace and faith to do just that. In so doing, it will be a great year!

The Spoken Word

(PART 2)

John 6:63 "It is the spirit that giveth life; the flesh profits nothing. The words that I speak unto you, they are spirit and they are life."

Our emphasis for the past several weeks is on our Lord and his mighty power as the Word of God, whether living, spoken, or written. As we continue to study his spoken Word, consider the following:

The healing power of the spoken Word.

Psalm 107:20 "He sent His Word and healed them and delivered them from their destructions." This verse gives evidence of the awesome power of the spoken Word of God. As I consider this truth, I am reminded of the many friends for whom we pray regularly and realize when the Lord chooses to heal, as he has done in many cases, he does it by a simple spoken Word. Does he always heal? No, but can he heal? Absolutely—with just a spoken word. We need to remember he is sovereign, and for his own purposes, he sometimes elects not to heal, as was the case with Apostle Paul. Our responsibility is to trust him and go to him in prayer, believing him to perform miracles of healing as he has so graciously done with family and friends.

The faith of a centurion.

Matthew 8:5–8 "And when Jesus was entered into Capernaum, there came unto Him a centurion, beseeching Him and saying, Lord my servant lieth at home sick with the palsy, grievously tormented. And Jesus said unto him, I will come and heal him. The centurion answered and said, Lord, I am not worthy that thou should come under my roof; but speak the word only, and my servant shall be healed."

Here is the centurion, a Gentile, having authority over one hundred men, with a great faith in the Lord Jesus and his ability to heal with just a spoken word. His faith made a great impression upon our Lord who was ministering, at the time, to the Jews, his chosen people. "When Jesus heard it, He marveled and said to them that followed, verily I say unto you, I have not found so great faith no not in Israel" (Matthew 8:10).

The power of his word over demons.

In the synagogue, there was a demon-possessed man. The demon cried out to Jesus to leave them alone. "And Jesus rebuked him saying, Hold thy peace and come out of him. And when the demon had thrown him down in the midst, he came out of him and hurt him not. And they were all amazed and spoke among themselves, saying, What a word is this! For with authority and power he commanded the unclean spirits and they came out" (Luke 4:33–35).

As I read these passages and see the incredible power of God at work in the lives of people, I can but wonder, why are we so faithless? Granted, we were not present when these miracles of Jesus were performed. We did not hear with physical ears his spoken Word but, we have his written Word, inspired by the Holy Spirit, which authenticates the truth of these miracles. Have our hearts grown cold and faithless? Would that we were like those "amazed by the power of His spoken Word."

Lord, send a revival, and let it begin in me.

Our Commander in Chief

Psalm 43:5 "Why are you cast down, O my soul? And why are you disquieted within me? Hope in God; for I shall yet praise him, who is the health of my countenance, and my God."

In the divided states of America, we hear, on one hand, how some have high hopes and expectations while others are quite concerned over the future of America. Within the latter group, we find fear and anxiety, worry, and even despair. The uncertainty of the future of our country, which goes far beyond the economy, should be a prayerful concern for all of us.

While many of our concerns are well founded, as believers, we need to remember who is in charge; commit our lives to him afresh and anew and claim his unfailing promises in these distressing times. "The Lord will not cast off his people, neither will he forsake his inheritance" (Psalm 94:14). Ultimately, every individual, as well as every nation, will bow before Almighty God and give glory to his holy name. "Be still and know that I am God; I will be exalted among the nations, I will be exalted in the earth" (Psalm 46:10).

While millions of God's children have been engaged in prayer for our nation these past months, it is no time for us to let up. I believe prayer is more needful than ever and one of our greatest weapons against the forces of evil at work in our land. May I encourage us to pray specifically; keeping our eyes on the Lord and our ears tuned in to current events. To be informed is to be forewarned. We need to be sensitive to God's Holy Spirit and develop the spirit of discernment, which can be a great asset when in spiritual warfare. We can, in faith, depend on the Holy Spirit to help us in our prayer life. "Likewise, the

Spirit also helps our infirmity; for we know not what we should pray for as we ought; but the Spirit himself makes intercession for us with groanings which cannot be uttered" (Romans 8:26).

May I challenge each of us to pray for our leaders, including the president, Congress, the Senate, the Supreme Court, and all in authority over us. For those who may be bitter or angry at our elected officials, this will not be easy, but not only are we commanded to do so, but I believe God will honor our obedience, and our prayers can be effective. "I exhort, therefore, that first of all, supplications, prayers, intercessions and giving of thanks be made for all men. For kings and for all that are in authority, that we may lead a quiet and peaceful life in all godliness and honesty" (1 Timothy 2:1–2). While some are totally at odds with what we believe and practice, I am reminded of the words of Jesus, "Love your enemies, do good to them who hate you, bless them that curse you and pray for them who despitefully use you" (Luke 6:27–28).

Issues to Consider

Matthew 12:25 "Every kingdom divided against
itself is brought to desolation; and every city or
house divided against itself shall not stand."

A Divided Nation

Like many great biblical truths, this one should sound a clear
alarm to us. Our country cannot continue on its present course
and survive much longer; it is greatly divided at the core. We may
be considered the only "world power" at this time, but our military might not prevail over time unless and until we come back to
God as a nation. The Bible says, "Not by might, nor by power, but
by my Spirit, saith the Lord of hosts" (Zechariah 4:6b). Without
Almighty God, we are powerless and cannot accomplish anything
worthwhile. Biblical history shows us what happens to individuals
and nations who turn away from worshipping and serving Jehovah
God. For example, consider this word concerning Israel. Psalm 99:8
"Thou answered them O Lord our God; thou were a God who for-
gavest them, though thou have taken vengeance on their misdeeds."
Individuals and nations, Christian or unsaved, will not get by with
sin. There is judgment against all sin. While the Lord Jesus took
our sin on Calvary along with its penalty, there is still a reckoning
for willful disobedience, that even Christians will be accountable to
God. A gross misconception that we as believers have is that we can
get away with sin. There will be consequences to us in this life as we
can see regarding Israel in the above verse.

Separation of Church and State

Historians, both Christian and non-Christian, have proven from history that the framers of our Constitution never intended for it to be interpreted as many are doing today. Our founding fathers, many who were believers in Christ, and God-fearing men, simply did not want a state religion. In fact, I believe our Constitution, along with the Declaration of Independence, are interwoven in their content with biblical truths and principals, including the Ten Commandments. God was in the very center of what they did as opposed to the effort by some today to remove every reference to the Almighty from our judicial system, our laws, our schools, and our society as a whole.

We may be called upon very soon to make tough choices.

Congress put together a so-called "hate crimes bill." In its original makeup, the bill would consider speaking out against the homosexual lifestyle, a hate crime. Such a bill would challenge our right to free speech. I do not want to use the "Word" to get into politics but only bring this up for those unaware of where this country is going. It is my firm belief, if God does not intervene on behalf of his people, we as Christians, already hated by many in our society, will face great challenges to our faith. We are responsible to God to obey the law, but I am suggesting for your consideration, there may come a time when our Christian liberties could be completely diminished.

The early disciples went about preaching the Gospel of Christ, and it caused anger both in the religious community as well as in the society of that day. You recall they were taken to prison; they were beaten and warned not to preach or teach any longer in the name of Jesus. I love their response. "Then Peter and the other apostles answered and said, we ought to obey God rather than men," (Acts 5:29). Wonder what our response would be should that be our plight!

Issues to Consider (continued)

First Timothy 2:1–2 "I exhort, therefore, that first of all, supplications, prayers, intercessions and giving of thanks be made for all men. For kings and all that are in authority, that we may lead a quiet and peaceable life in all godliness and honesty."

Our Leaders

Regardless of our political preference, the Bible makes it perfectly clear what the Christian's duty is toward those in office. Sometimes it is a challenge to pray for those with whom we may disagree, but like it or not, we are clearly commanded to do just that. In the last several decades, the Office of the President has been abused by leaders from both political parties. This has further led to a great division in our country. Unpopular wars, illegal and immoral actions have fueled the flames of discontent in our nation for many, many years. While we should all be thankful for the freedom of speech and the right to disagree with our leaders, as Christians, we can disagree without being disagreeable and continue to show respect for the high offices of our elected officials. The lies, abuse, criticism, slander, and pure hatred exemplified by many today for those in high office are unlike anything I have witnessed in my lifetime. I wonder what would happen in our country if every Christian would obey God's command in Timothy.

The Bible reminds us in Romans 13:1–2 "Let every soul be subject unto the higher powers. For there is no power but of God; the powers that be are ordained of God. Whosoever, therefore, resisteth the power, resisteth the ordinance of God; and they that resist shall receive to themselves judgment." Based on the actions of many in our society today, there is serious judgment coming to some.

Corrupt Officials and Legal Rulings

"He that justifieth the wicked, and he that condemneth the just, even they both are an abomination to the Lord" (Proverbs 17:15).

We have watched first in shock, disbelief, and then in anger as our Congress proposed laws that have protected the guilty and did little or nothing for the victimized and the innocent. So often we see everything from white-collar crimes to predators of women and children all the way to murder—result in nothing more in the way of a penalty than a slap on the wrist or a few months in jail. The wicked seem to be justified while it is as though the just are condemned and receive no justice. The movie and television industry are, at will, sending into our homes violence, sex, and profanity, which should be checked and stopped by the FCC. One can hardly watch the news without lewd, suggestive commercials that should not be allowed on TV. Our children's and grandchildren's minds are being affected by this and the filth they call music coming across the airwaves.

Oh, that Christians would rise up and say "enough is enough," but we passively ignore the deterioration of all that is right and good in our society. There is a word for us found in Proverbs 24:24–25 "He that saith unto the wicked, thou are righteous; him shall the people curse, nations shall abhor him; but to those who rebuke him shall be delight, and a good blessing shall come upon them." Our society condones immorality and attempts to convince us that anything goes. May God help us, first of all, to be sure our walk with the Lord is pleasing to him and then may we prayerfully but with holy boldness rebuke the works of darkness.

Issues to Consider

Corrupt Judges and Politicians

> Isaiah 10:1–2 "Woe unto them who decree unrighteous
> decrees, and who write grievousness which they have
> prescribed, to turn away the needy from justice and to take
> away the right from the poor of my people, that widows
> may be their prey and that they may rob the fatherless."

Our nation, like Israel of Isaiah's day, is experiencing the same corruption among politicians and judges. Many judges across our land are not enforcing our laws, but they are changing them and making decisions that affect us all, based on their own preferences and interpretations. For decades now, politicians have lied to and deceived the poor and needy. While professing to really care, they have taught generations of the poor, fatherless and uneducated, to totally depend upon the federal government in order to gain their political support. Talk about identify theft! Through their deceptive practices, they are robbing people of their dignity and self-worth. Our inability to teach or even discuss in our public schools the truths of God's Word and his love for all people regardless of race, color, or creed is what I believe to be a major factor in the moral decay of our society. To an extent, the souls of our children are being stolen. There is another appropriate word from the Lord that, while originally intended for Israel, is so descriptive of America in 2015. It could be the headline on *USA Today*. Isaiah 59:14–15 "Justice is turned away backward and righteousness standeth afar off; for truth is fallen in the street, and equity cannot enter. Yea, truth faileth and he that departeth from evil maketh himself a prey. And the Lord saw it and it displeased Him that there was no justice."

What a vivid description as to where we are today as a nation. Truth as we know it is missing in our society, which calls evil good and good evil. Note those who are sincere in wanting to walk with the Lord and depart from every appearance of evil, make themselves a prey. Do you ever recall a time in life when God-fearing, Bible-believing Christians were so despised and hated by so many? Proverbs 17:15 "He that justifieth the wicked and he that condemneth the just, even they both are an abomination to the Lord."

While we do not expect a lost and dying world to change, God does want and, I believe, expect his people to repent of sin and seek him with our hearts so that in his mercy, he would bring revival to us, and our nation would turn from destruction. Isaiah 59:1–4 "Behold the Lord's hand is not shortened, that it cannot save; neither His ear heavy, that it cannot hear. But your iniquities have separated between you and your God and your sins have hidden His face from you, that He will not hear. For your hands are defiled with blood and your fingers with iniquity; your lips have spoken lies, your tongue has muttered perverseness. None calleth for justice, nor any pleadeth for truth; they trust in vanity and speak lies; they conceive mischief and bring forth iniquity."

Change That Can Make A Difference

Proverbs 4:23 "Keep your heart with all diligence,
for out of it spring the issues of life."

Much has been said these past several years in the political arena about change. America as a nation certainly needs change, but the change we need is a moral one. All of our problems as individuals and as a nation are issues of the heart. The Bible, through Jeremiah the Prophet, describes us well. "The heart is deceitful above all things and desperately wicked; who can know it?" (Jeremiah 17:9).

As we look back at this past year, are there not many things in our lives which we would like to do a lot better? I am not addressing New Year's resolutions, but real change that begins in our hearts. What better time to start fresh with the Lord than at the beginning of a new year. The first thing we must do is acknowledge to our Heavenly Father our sins and shortcomings. We have several wonderful promises we can claim. "If we confess our sins, He is faithful and just to forgive us our sins and to cleanse us from all unrighteousness" (1 John 1:9). Many times, we want the forgiveness but not the cleansing. The scripture clearly says we need both. "He who covers his sins will not prosper, but whoever confesses and forsakes them will have mercy" (Proverbs 28:13). What a glorious way to start the new year—with a clean heart!

I love the way David prayed, "Create in me a clean heart, O God, and renew a steadfast spirit within me" (Psalm 51:10). Please observe again we not only need a clean heart, which signifies the cleansing, but a steadfast spirit. In other words, by God's grace, we want change in our hearts to be faithful and true to our Lord. This is a full-time responsibility for each of us, keeping our heart right with all diligence. The rewards of our efforts are many, however, well worth our every effort. What greater joy is there than to walk with the Lord in fellowship every day? Upon being forgiven and cleansed, we need to join Paul then in saying, "Forgetting those things that are behind and reaching forward to those things which are ahead, I press toward the goal for the prize of the upward call of God in Jesus Christ" (Philippians 3:13). Do not dwell on past sins and failures or allow Satan to throw them up to you. The past belongs to God. After confessing, leave them with the Lord. Hebrews 9:11–15 tells us how the precious blood of Christ cleanses our conscience from dead works so we are able to serve the living God.

The wonderful thing is the Lord longs to be in close fellowship with each of us and has provided in Christ the means for us to do just that. The Word encourages us to "draw near with a true heart in full assurance of faith" (Hebrews 10:22). Then again in James 4:8, "Draw near to God and He will draw near to you." Notice the first move is ours. We have to desire from our heart to be close to the Lord. I close with the invitation from Jesus himself, "Come unto me, all you who labor and are heavy laden, and I will give you rest. Take my yoke upon you and learn of me; for I am meek and lowly in heart, and you shall find rest for your souls. For my yoke is easy, and my burden is light" (Matthew 11:28–30).

Hope for America

Second Chronicles 7:14 "If my people who are called by
My name will humble themselves, and pray and seek My
face, and turn from their wicked ways, then I will hear from
heaven, and will forgive their sin and heal their land."

For several weeks, we have considered our divided nation and the forces of evil at work in society. We have determined that at the heart of the problem is none other than Satan, the old serpent, the devil himself! His influence on our people, saved or lost, is indisputable and far-reaching—from the affluent and powerful, beginning in Washington, to the peasants on the streets of America. As we observe, before our very eyes, the moral, ethical, political, and economic collapse of our country, we can but wonder, is there any hope at all? Can America be restored?

As people of faith, we know that as long as God permits, through his mercy, love, and grace, we have hope for the future and revival among his children. We cannot sit idly by, however, and continue to conform to the world and its ways. The Bible admonishes us to "come out from among them and be separate, says the Lord. Do not touch what is unclean and I will receive you, I will be a Father to you, and you shall be my sons and daughters, says the Lord Almighty" (2 Corinthians 6:17).

A wonderful place for us to start is by claiming the promise of our text verse, 2 Chronicles 7:14. This verse is most likely familiar to us, but I hope its familiarity would not cause us to take it lightly. The verse offers a sure hope to us as individuals and as a nation. It is imperative to note, however, the conjunction *if*. It clearly signifies this to be a conditional promise of God. Our Heavenly Father promises to heal our land only if you and I commit to fulfilling the requirements of the promise.

The promise is not directed to all Americans, but specifically to believers. "My people who are called by My name." We cannot pass the blame to those who are lost. Throughout biblical history, God deals in and through his people. Our obedience to the Lord in keeping his Word directly impacts not only our lives and our families but our very nation. So does our disobedience!

The name of the Lord is sacred and holy, and we have taken it lightly, neglecting to honor his holy name by our unholy lifestyles. It is my personal belief that as Christians, we are reaping today what we have sown. We are paying the price for our sin! "Do not be deceived, God is not mocked, for whatsoever a man sows, that he will also reap" (Galatians 6:7).

The Truth Shall Set You Free

Second Timothy 4:3–4 "For the time will come when they will not endure sound doctrine but, after their own lusts, shall they heap to themselves teachers, having itching ears; and they shall turn away their ears from the truth and shall be turned unto fables."

When Apostle Paul wrote this letter to young Timothy, he said the "time will come." My friends, as I write today, the time has come! It is evident in many areas of Christendom that we no longer adhere to sound doctrine. In an alarming, but not at all surprising, study, Barna learned that there is a profound lack of belief in the essential Christian doctrine. For example, of non-denominational churches, only 70 percent believe the Bible is totally accurate while only 66 percent of Baptists believe it to be accurate. Less than 50 percent of all professing Christians believe Satan is real, and across most denominational lines, 40 percent or better believe good works can earn an entrance into heaven.

The Bible clearly says, "For by grace are you saved through faith; and that not of yourselves, it is the gift of God, not of works, lest any man should boast" (Ephesians 2:8–9). To believe otherwise is heresy! If man could work his way into heaven, then Jesus died in vain, but he knew his atoning death on Calvary was the only way sinful, lost, and depraved man could ever be redeemed. In fact, he clearly stated, "I am the way, the truth, and the life; no man cometh unto the Father but by me" (John 14:6).

The hellish pride of man refuses to accept the truth of the Gospel, and without repentance of sin and faith in the finished work of the Lord Jesus Christ on Calvary, he will die in his sin and spend eternity in a devil's hell, which at the moment he may not even believe exists. One thing is certain; he will believe one second after he breathes his last breath.

In today's society, people want to hear feel-good teaching and preaching. Itching ears turned away from the truth. New age teaching denies the divinity of the Lord Jesus, the existence of sin and hell, and is teaching lies across this nation to countless thousands of followers whose blood will be on their hands at the Great White Throne Judgment in eternity!

The Bible alerts us to this truth, "Little children, it is in the last time; and as you have heard that Anti-Christ shall come, even now are there many Anti-Christs, by which we know that it is the last time" (1 John 2:18). In these last days, our churches are filled with people who not only fail to adhere to sound doctrine but have no idea what they believe or why they believe it. Many are members of a church but not members of the Body of Christ. Born of the flesh, but not of the Spirit. Sad is the case when at the Judgment, they stand before the King of Kings and Lord of Lords, telling him all the "good works" they have done, only to hear those piercing words, "Depart from me you cursed into everlasting fire, prepared for the Devil and his angels" (Matthew 25:41).

I pray that no one reading this today will make the mistake of going into eternity without knowing beyond a doubt that he or she has placed their faith in the Lord Jesus Christ. "Knowing that a man is not justified by the works of the law, but by the faith of Jesus Christ, even we have believed in Jesus Christ that we might be justified by the faith of Christ and not by the works of the law; for by the works of the law shall no flesh be justified" (Galatians 2:16).

Fear Not

Isaiah 41:10 "Fear not, for I am with you; be not dismayed, for I am your God. I will strengthen you, yes, I will help you, I will uphold you with my righteous right hand."

As I write this Monday morning, our nation is being threatened by Islamic extremist rebels from Somalia. In a video, they call on Muslims to attack us in our malls and, in particular, the Mall of America in Bloomington, Minnesota. While the FBI says there is no evidence of a credible threat at this time, I am certain this will strike fear in many hearts across our land, which is one of the objectives of these terrorists. Make no mistake, my friends, their ultimate objective is world dominance!

As believers, let us not ask why this is happening, but rather, let us prayerfully ask our Lord what he is trying to teach us. Personally, I strongly believe this is but another evidence that we are living in the Last Days before the return of the Lord, to rapture his Church out of this wicked sin-cursed world. The Bible gives us numerous warnings of the Last Days such as in 2 Timothy 3:1, "But know this, that in the last days perilous times will come!" Allow me to encourage you to finish reading this chapter through verse 7.

Is it possible that God is giving believers a wake-up call? I certainly believe he is. Throughout the New Testament, the admonition to each of us is to watch and wait. For example, the parable of the ten virgins ends with these words, "Watch therefore for you know neither the day or the hour in which the Son of Man is coming" (Matthew 25:13). In the meantime, we are to be salt and light in an evil world destined for an eternal hell of fire!

For those of us in Christ, there is no need to fear. As our text from Isaiah says, "Fear not for I am with thee." What a great assurance for these troubled times. Our Omnipotent Creator, our Savior and Lord, is with us, and he promised he would never leave us or forsake us. He is the Alpha and the Omega, the Beginning and the End, the great "I Am." Just imagine the same Almighty God, who called Moses to lead his people out of bondage through his mighty acts of power, is the same God who is giving us strength, assurance, and hope in his ability to uphold each of us with his righteous right hand. Our job is to claim his promise, live each day by faith, and trust him with all of our hearts in the midst of life's storms. Psalm 62:5 through 8 says, "My soul, wait silently for God alone, for my expectation is from Him. He only is my rock and my salvation; He is my defense; I shall not be moved. In God is my salvation and my glory; the rock of my strength and my refuge, is in God. Trust in Him at all times, you people, pour out your heart before Him; God is a refuge for us." Take courage.

Law and Grace Cannot Coexist

Genesis 21:9–10 "And Sarah saw the son of Hagar the Egyptian, whom she had borne unto Abraham, mocking. Wherefore she said unto Abraham, cast out this bondwoman and her son; for the son of this bondwoman shall not be heir with my son, even with Isaac."

In obedience to the Lord and as a sign of the covenant between them, "Abraham circumcised his son Isaac being eight days old, as God had commanded him" (Genesis 21:4). Then as evidence that things of the flesh cannot co-exist with those of the spirit, trouble arises. As our text outlines, Ishmael, Abraham's son of the flesh mocks, causing Sarah to become angry and desires he be cast out. Sarah makes the significant statement that Ishmael shall not be heir with Isaac, the son of promise. This is difficult for Abraham, who loves Ishmael. Nevertheless, he follows God's instruction to do as Sarah has requested (Genesis 21:9–21).

We are reminded even today, how difficult it is sometimes for Christians to let go of fleshly desires and ambitions and walk daily in the spirit. The apostle Paul addresses this ongoing problem in Galatians 5:17: "For the flesh lusteth against the Spirit, and the Spirit against the flesh; and these are contrary the one to the other, so that you cannot do the things that you would." Our churches today are filled with good-intention Christians trying desperately to live the Christian life in the power of the flesh, which is virtually impossible. The answer to walking and living in the spirit is made clear in God's Word. Galatians 2:20, "I am crucified with Christ; nevertheless I live; yet not I, but Christ liveth in me; and the life which I now live in the flesh I live by the faith of the Son of God, who loved me and gave himself for me."

A foundational truth of our faith is at the heart of this conflict between Ishmael and Isaac. Ishmael represents the law given at Mt. Sinai while Isaac, the son of promise, represents grace and salvation available to all who will come to God in repentance of sin and faith in the Lord Jesus Christ. Outside of true Christianity, the religions of the world identify with Ishmael trying vainly to somehow earn salvation by the works of the flesh. Sadly enough, even many professing Christians totally misunderstand the truth in "knowing that a man is not justified by the works of the law, but by the faith of Jesus Christ, even we have believed in Jesus Christ, that we might be justified by the faith of Christ, and not by the works of the law; for by the works of the law shall no flesh be justified" (Galatians 2:16).

On the other hand, what a wonderful assurance we have as believers for "Now we, brethren, as Isaac was, are the children of promise" (Galatians 4:28). Through faith in Christ by God's amazing grace, we though Gentiles by nature, are sons of Abraham. Galatians 3:7–9 "Know you, therefore, that they who are of faith, the same are sons of Abraham. And the scripture, foreseeing that God would justify the Gentiles through faith, preached before the Gospel unto Abraham, saying, "In thee shall all nations be blessed. So, then, they who are of faith are blessed with faithful Abraham."

A Willing Sacrifice

Genesis 22:7–8 "And Isaac spoke unto Abraham, his father, and said, my father; and he said, here am I, my son. And he said, behold the fire and the wood: but where is the lamb for a burnt offering? And Abraham said, my son, God will provide himself a lamb for a burnt offering; so they went both of them together."

Isaac is not a child now but a young man. While we do not know his exact age, he is old enough to resist being offered as a sacrifice once he realizes he is to be the burnt offering. Isaac chose, however, to be submissive to God and his earthly father, Abraham, allowing himself to be bound by his aged father and was obedient even unto death. Likewise, Abraham, a loving father, who would gladly give his own life to save his son, does not allow his human love or emotions to prevail over his faith and obedience to Jehovah God. What a beautiful illustration to us! Abraham, for example, is a type of our Heavenly Father, who, according to Romans 8:32a, "spared not his own Son, but delivered Him up for us all." A Heavenly Father whose unequaled, matchless love for a lost and dying world was exemplified when he sent his one and only Son to die for our sin on Calvary's tree. "For God so loved the world that he gave His only begotten Son that whosoever believeth in Him should not perish but have everlasting life" (John 3:16).

Isaac was, in many ways, a type of Christ. The Virgin Mary was overshadowed by the Holy Spirit and conceived in her womb the Lord Jesus; "And behold, thou shalt conceive in thy womb, and bring forth a son, and shalt call His name Jesus" (Luke 1:31). Though certainly not in the same manner, but miraculous in itself, was Sarah's conception of Isaac. "Through faith also Sarah herself received strength to conceive seed, and was delivered of a child when she was past age, because she judged Him faithful who had promised" (Hebrews 11:11).

Then as was stated earlier, we see Isaac as a type of Christ willing to be sacrificed. The Bible says of our Lord Jesus, "Being found in fashion as a man, He humbled Himself and became obedient unto death, even the death of the cross" (Philippians 2:8). In the case of Isaac, the Lord provided a substitute in his place, to be sacrificed. A ram caught in the thicket (Genesis 22:13). The Lord Jesus was our substitute. He was offered as the once-for-all sacrifice of the new covenant in our stead (Hebrews 10:1–18). It is impossible for man to obtain salvation any other way but through the precious blood of Jesus, which was shed for us on the cross. "For as much as you know that you were not redeemed with corruptible things ... but with the precious blood of Christ, as of a lamb without blemish and without spot" (1 Peter 1:18–19). Then the typology is confirmed in Hebrews 11:17–19 because Abraham believed God would raise Isaac from the dead after he was sacrificed "from which he received him in a figure."

After paying in full for our sin, Jesus was buried in the tomb of Joseph of Arimathea until three days later when Mary Magdalene and the other Mary came to see the sepulcher. "And the angel said unto them ... 'Fear not; for I know that you seek Jesus, who was crucified. He is not here; for He is risen as He said'" (Matthew 28:5–6). As a result of His humbling Himself and becoming obedient unto death, even the death of the cross, a willing sacrifice, our Lord Jesus is "able also to save them to the uttermost that come unto God by him, seeing he ever liveth to make intercession for them" (Hebrews 7:25). All praise, glory, and honor be unto the Lamb who sits on the throne of the Majesty on High!

Divine Revelation

Luke 10:21 "In that hour Jesus rejoiced in the Spirit, and said, I thank thee, O Father, Lord of heaven and earth, that thou hast hidden these things from the wise and prudent, and hast revealed them unto babes, even so, Father; for so it seemed good in thy sight."

In the tenth chapter of Luke, the Lord sends out an additional seventy believers to heal the sick and proclaim the good news of the kingdom of God. Following this, the Lord denounces several major cities of that day—Chorazin, Bethsaida, and Capernaum—because of their unbelief and rejection of the Lord Himself. He warns of the coming judgment upon them. As the seventy return, rejoicing at the results of their ministry for the Lord, he offers encouragement and the beautiful prayer in Luke 10:21, our text verse.

Wisdom can be a wonderful asset to a godly Christian who will use it for God's glory. Education and higher learning can be a blessing when coupled with the knowledge of God's Word and will. On the other hand, worldly knowledge gained from books or from the teaching of those who do not profess to know the Lord, can not only be harmful but even dangerous. God only knows how many young minds have been led astray and confused by those who deny God, the creation, and count the Bible but a book of myths. Psalm 14:1 "The fool has said in his heart, there is no God."

How thankful we should be for the simplicity of the Gospel of Christ, its redemptive message, and the fact that it is totally by grace that the Father revealed its truth to every believer. It was Jesus who said, "Permit little children to come unto me, and forbid them not;

for of such is the Kingdom of God. Verily, I say unto you, whosoever shall not receive the Kingdom of God like a little child shall in no way enter it" (Luke 18:16–17). We are indeed blessed to have heard the good news "that Christ died for our sins according to the Scriptures; and that he was buried, and that he rose again the third day according to the Scriptures" (1 Corinthians 3a–4). The Gospel message is so profound and powerful. Paul refers to it as "the power of God unto salvation to everyone that believeth" (Romans 1:16). It is the power of God that transforms the lives of men, women, boys, and girls—to all those whom he chooses to reveal the Gospel message and will accept it.

May we never take our salvation for granted. We need to thank the Lord regularly for revealing to us the way of salvation because to many of the wise of this world, it is hidden. This relationship with our Lord carries an enormous responsibility for each of us like the seventy he sent out to share the good news with family and friends and to intercede for their salvation. "Awake to righteousness, and sin not; for some have not the knowledge of God. I speak this to your shame," (1 Corinthians 1:34). May we plant the seed by sharing our faith, water it with tears of concern, and trust God for the increase of souls.

A Lesson from Life

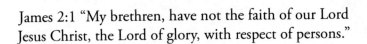

James 2:1 "My brethren, have not the faith of our Lord
Jesus Christ, the Lord of glory, with respect of persons."

A young eighteen-year-old sailor stepped off the train in
Jacksonville, Florida, with his new bride of the same age and
one large metal trunk that contained all of their earthly possessions.
Checking the trunk at the railroad station to be picked up later, they
purchased a newspaper and a map of the city. Although he had been
stationed at the US Naval Air Base in Jacksonville for about one year,
his knowledge of the city was limited as he had rarely left the base.

Not owning a car, they rode the bus to look for a modest place
to live. It was as though the Lord led them to a two-story home
located on Post Street where the landlord and his wife lived on the
lower floor, renting out the upstairs to two separate tenants. The couple was delighted with the two-room apartment with a bath "down
the hall." The fifty-dollar monthly rent represented 25 percent of
their total monthly income.

Having professed faith in Christ only a short time prior, they
were anxious to find a church where they could attend. There was a
sign on the corner where they lived, pointing down the street where
several blocks away was Woodlawn Baptist Church. They attended
the following Sunday morning. Neither had ever been active in a
church although coming from a Catholic background, his bride
attended Mass regularly. Even though neither had ever sung in a
church choir, they joined almost immediately. It was a small church
of about three or four hundred members and the pastor was Brother
Sanders.

The way the church received this struggling young couple was nothing less than an amazing act of love and grace. The pastor, his wife, and children, also young marrieds, not only took them into their home for social gatherings on occasion but, more importantly, into their hearts. In addition, several families reached out to them in love. On the nights he had duty at the base, a young couple, just a bit older than they, came and picked up the young bride and let her stay overnight in their home so she would not be alone in a strange city. I am reminded here of the words of Jesus, "By this shall all men know that you are my disciples, if you have love one to another" (John 13:35).

After completing his remaining nine months in service, the young man and his now six-months-pregnant wife would return to their home in Louisiana, but not before these new friends gave them a beautiful baby shower. The words of James come to mind from the second chapter, verse 18, "A man may say, thou has faith, and I have works; show me thy faith without thy works and I will show you my faith by my works."

It is hard to know what the preaching was like at Woodlawn Baptist Church, perhaps not very evangelistic or profound, maybe even quite ordinary, we might say. Having grown accustomed to a large church and choir, the irony is, even if it were possible to bring back that same church with its same pastor and membership, I cannot say that after all this time if my bride of fifty years and I would consider joining that small church.

One cannot help but wonder, however, when we get so wrapped up in our own church and fellowship, how many "Brother Sanders" and small congregations, which we drive by every day, are serving our Lord and meeting the needs of His children. It also opens one's eyes to those around us in our own congregation, who may be struggling, hurting, and just needing someone to care and show them love.

We have been in many great churches during the past fifty years, but none has left a more indelible impression upon our lives than the one we attended for only nine months—Woodlawn Baptist Church! A congregation indeed where there were no respecters of persons.

Jesus vs. Religion

Matthew 18:3 "Verily I say unto you, except you
be converted and become as little children you
shall not enter into the kingdom of heaven."

Throughout his earthly ministry, Jesus encountered opposition from the religious leaders of his day. The two major groups were the Sadducees and the Pharisees. The Sadducees denied the resurrection and made the mistake of trying to deceive the Lord with a question (Matthew 22:23–33). The Pharisees, though believing in the resurrection, had abandoned the truth of God's Word and set up their own long list of religious rules. Jesus warned his followers of their false doctrine.

"Then Jesus said unto them, take heed and beware of the leaven of the Pharisees and of the Sadducees. Then understood they that He bade them not to beware of the leaven of bread but of the doctrine of the Pharisees and of the Sadducees" (Matthew 16:6, 12).

After his triumphant entry into Jerusalem, the Lord "went into the temple of God and cast out all them that sold and bought in the temple and overthrew the tables of the moneychangers and the seats of them that sold doves. And said unto them, it is written, my house shall be called a house of prayer, but you have made it a den of thieves" (Matthew 21:12–13). The actions of the religious leaders proved how religion without regeneration and a personal relationship with Christ is empty, cold, and meaningless. A further look at the crowd proves that theirs was a problem of an unregenerate heart. "You hypocrites, well did Isaiah prophesy of you, saying, this people draweth near unto me with their mouth and honoreth me with their lips, but their heart is far from me. But in vain they do worship me, teaching for doctrines the commandments of men" (Matthew 15:7–9).

Religion in and of itself cannot provide eternal life, forgiveness of sin, or purpose for life and living. In fact, trusting in religion rather than Christ to save you will only result in one being lost for eternity and banished to a hell of fire without God and without hope. Sadly enough, churches of all denominations are filled with people today who are staking their eternal destiny on some religious beliefs or practices. Religious, yes, but *lost!* It is possible to be a faithful church member, teacher or deacon, to believe in one's head about Christ and His resurrection and still be unsaved. As our text verse says, we must be converted (born again) and with a childlike faith, trust Christ to be Savior and Lord. As the Bible says, "That if thou shalt confess with thy mouth the Lord Jesus and shall believe in thine heart that God has raised him from the dead, thou shall be saved. For with the heart man believeth unto righteousness and with the mouth confession is made unto salvation. For the scripture saith whosoever believeth on him shall not be ashamed" (Romans 10:9–11).

Identity Theft

John 10:10a "The thief cometh not but to
steal and to kill and to destroy."

One of the latest and fast-growing crimes in America today is identity theft. It is a disparaging crime that preys on the innocent; steals one's name, credit, reputation, resources, integrity, peace, joy, and, for a time, one's very purpose. I sympathize with anyone who has been so victimized.

Far more concerning to me is the ongoing theft of America's identity. Who are we anyway? We still profess to be "a Christian nation" who believes in Almighty God, but if we are, we have lost our witness, our effectiveness. Yes, even our purpose. No longer are we the United States, but a country so divided that our identity has been lost. Are we the Bible-believing, God-fearing people who are committed to our Lord and Savior, Jesus Christ, seeking to influence a lost and dying world? Or are we the secular, humanist society, perverted, debased, parading openly our sin and shame, defying God and everything that is right and moral while we are infatuated with the acquisition of material things, sports, sex, violence, and the pleasures of a world lost and going to hell? Those of us in our senior years find the great country we served and love has been transformed into a nation we no longer recognize. Our founding fathers would be in shock and disbelief to see our country in its current condition.

As a sculptor would chisel and chip away at a piece of stone to create a carving or monument, the forces of evil are steadily chipping away at the moral fiber of our country with the ultimate objective to steal its very soul. Presently, if we are honest, the forces of evil are winning, for the very principles that once made our country great are eroding before our very eyes. Our society ignores divine truth; you can do anything you want to do no matter how appalling or shocking it is, and that is okay and acceptable. Right has become wrong, and wrong has been accepted as right. Our forefathers set out to establish freedoms and liberties for us to enjoy; these came at a high price. Many died for the freedoms we have enjoyed, but our enemies are using these liberties to destroy us. Sadly enough, many of our citizens are blinded from the truth. Second Corinthians 4:3–4 "If our gospel be hidden it is hidden to them that are lost, in whom the God of this world has blinded the minds of them who believe not, lest the light of the glorious gospel of Christ, who is the image of God, should shine unto them."

The Lord has laid on my heart for some time now, the plight of our nation. Consequently, I want to share with you some biblical truths that address the problems we face, and hope that we will be impressed by the Lord, individually and collectively to earnestly and fervently pray for revival in our country. Our only hope as a nation is a revival among the people of God and a spiritual awakening. May I encourage you that the 120 people in an upper room, filled with God's Holy Spirit, committed totally to the Lord and sharing the Gospel, turned their world upside down. Numerically we have half that many, which we know of receiving this word, not to mention a remnant across our nation, which only God can number, who are praying for our country. The point is you and I can make a difference by praying. James 5:16 "The effectual, fervent prayer of a righteous man availeth much."

A Matter of the Heart

Proverbs 4:23 "Keep your heart with all diligence,
for out of it spring the issues of life."

It is possible for us to be diligent in many things such as our family, vocation, finances, and even in the Lord's service and still miss the most important matter we should be diligent about—the keeping of our heart before God. When our heart is not right, everything else is out of place or out of order. Keeping one's heart attentive involves the presence and power of God in our lives, along with our personal commitment and discipline in the matter. There are multiple distractions in our society today that challenge every earnest effort on our part to live a holy, consecrated life for Christ.

The root of our problem is described well in Jeremiah 17:9, "The heart is deceitful above all things and desperately wicked; who can know it?" Add to that the words of Jesus who said, "Out of the heart proceed evil thoughts, murders, adulteries, fornications, thefts, false witness, blasphemies" (Matthew 15:19). This, to me, is why it is crucial for us to spend time in God's Word every day, praying for his strength and guidance. When we acknowledge our utter dependence upon him, through the power of the Holy Spirit we can have victory in our lives for "greater is He that is in you than he that is in the world" (1 John 4:4).

When we expose ourselves to the Word of God, the Holy Spirit shines his searchlight upon us to show us those things in our hearts that are displeasing to him. The Bible says, "The word of God is living and powerful and sharper than any two-edged sword, piercing even to the division of soul and spirit and of joints and marrow and is a discerner of the thoughts and intents of the heart" (Hebrews 4:12). God's Word not only brings conviction but shows us how to be forgiven and cleansed. It takes earnest effort on our part and the will to be obedient to God's Word. "How can a young man cleanse his way? By taking heed according to your word" (Psalm 119:9).

The good news is that God freely forgives our sin through the blood of Christ, as we confess to him but will with the asking, fill us with his Holy Spirit. Jesus said, "He who believes in Me, as the Scripture has said, out of his heart will flow rivers of living water" (John 7:38). Would it not be a marvelous experience being filled with the Holy Spirit of God, that he poured out of our hearts and lives living water to those in need? May God grant that to each of us for his glory!

Someone well said, "Sin will keep us from God's Word and God's Word will keep us from sin."

Be Alert

Luke 11:21 "When a strong man, fully armed,
guards his own palace, his goods are in peace."

In this passage, Jesus is referring to Satan and how he works to safeguard a false peace for those under his influence and control. In comparison to mortal man, he is very strong and protects the worldly domain he temporarily controls, using everything at his disposal. With his lies and deceptive spirit, he convinces lost man that all is well. Before our conversion, did not all of us have a false hope for eternity? We may have trusted religion, our heritage, good works, or false doctrine.

Those of us over fifty years of age can go back to the 1960s when we began to see the beginning of moral decline in our nation. Under the influence of the wicked one, some in society proclaimed "God is dead." Using anti-war rhetoric, we heard things like "make love, not war" and "if it feels good, do it." The whole idea behind the movement was to take God, accountability, and judgment out of the equation. This goes all the way back to the beginning of creation when Satan questioned Eve in the Garden as to what God really said. He is magnifying that same thing today. The Bible says, "But know this, that in the last days perilous times will come. For men will be lovers of themselves, lovers of money, boasters, proud, blasphemers, disobedient to parents, unthankful, unloving, unforgiving, slanderers, without self-control, brutal, despisers of good, traitors, headstrong, haughty, lovers of pleasure rather than lovers of God, having a form of godliness but denying its power" (2 Timothy 3:1–5).

Satan devised his plan to destroy America, and he is well on the way to doing just that. It was not always as obvious as it is today, but subtle and deliberate. Like a sculptor on a large stone working to shape it, Satan and his forces have chipped away at the moral fiber of America. His objective is to convince men and women that God and his Word are totally irrelevant in our society and at this time we are on a slippery slope leading to destruction. Satan is taking captives daily!

"A servant of the Lord must not quarrel but be gentle to all, able to teach, patient, in humility correcting those who are in opposition, if God perhaps will grant them repentance, so that they may know the truth, and that they may come to their senses and escape the snare of the devil, having been taken captive by him to do his will" (2 Timothy 2:24–26). Satan has taken captives of peasants and politicians, the rich and famous, and many unknown souls. We know he has come to steal, kill, and destroy. Therefore, to be forewarned is to be forearmed!

The Bible says, "If the master of the house had known what hour the thief would come, he would have watched and not allowed his house to be broken into" (Matthew 24:43). Will you stand in the gap with me for our families and our country? "I sought for a man among them who would make a wall, and stand in the gap before me on behalf of the land, that I should not destroy it; but I found no one" (Ezekiel 22:30).

Revealing the Enemy

Revelation 12:12 "Woe to the inhabitants of the earth and of the seal For the Devil is come down to you, having great wrath, because he knows that he has but a short time."

When our Lord Jesus Christ made the supreme sacrifice on Calvary, not only did he make atonement for sin, but he sealed the fate of Satan for eternity. The prophecy concerning the Lord and the adversary, Satan, was fulfilled. Genesis 3:15 "I will put enmity between you and the woman, and between your seed and her seed: He shall bruise your head, and you shall bruise his heel." True to the prophecy, we know Satan bruised the Lord through his mockery of a trial, his beatings, and the ultimate crucifixion, but when Jesus cried from the cross, "It is finished" (John 19:30), not only was the atonement completed, but Satan was forever defeated. The resurrection that followed three days later solidified God's acceptance of the redemptive act of our Lord and gave to every believer the assurance of victory over sin, death, and the grave.

Knowing he is a defeated foe and that his time is short, the wicked one is on a worldwide rampage in these last days. Jesus defines Satan as a liar and the author of it, whose motive is clear in John 10:10, "The thief comes not but to steal and to kill and to destroy." Satan is a liar, a deceiver, a thief, and a murderer.

We understand from scripture that when Adam sinned, he forfeited dominion over creation, which was given him by the Almighty God. Now, for a time, Satan is in control of this world system. Jesus referred to him as the prince of this world. "Hereafter I will not talk much with you; for the prince of this world comes, and has nothing in me" (John 14:30). Should there be any doubt of Satan's authority over the world system at this time, please study the temptation of Jesus in Matthew, chapter 4. In verse 8, Satan shows Jesus the kingdoms of the world and then in verse 9, he says, "All these things will I give you, if you will fall down and worship me." Of course, Jesus rebuked Satan through the Word of God, but do not miss the point. How could Satan offer the kingdoms of the world and the glory of them, except that he is in control for now?

Satan works in the hearts of lost men, just as he did in your heart and mine before we were saved. "And you has He made alive, who were dead in trespasses and sins; in which in times past you walked according to the course of this world, according to the prince of the power of the air, the spirit that now works in the sons of disobedience" (Ephesians 2:1–2). Do not underestimate the power of our enemy. We are no match for him in the flesh. Our defense is to be clothed in the armor of God as found in Ephesians, chapter 6, and most of all to be covered by the precious blood of Christ. "And they overcame him by the blood of the Lamb" (Revelation 12:11).

Please note it is very important to understand that the temporary power of Satan is within the permissive will of God and part of God's divine plan. God is sovereign and all powerful and in complete control!

An Earnest Prayer

Psalm 79:9 "Help us O God of our salvation, for the glory of your name; and deliver us and purge away our sins for your name's sake."

It is quite apparent today that America is in great spiritual need and the road we are traveling is a road leading to destruction. Many in our society believe the way we are going is right, but the Bible says, "There is a way which seems right to a man but the end thereof are the ways of death" (Proverbs 14:12). This is true for an individual and can be true for an entire nation. We desperately need to return to the Lord.

This movement has to initiate with the people of God who claim Christ Jesus as Lord and Savior. It requires a repentance of sin on our part, a return to godly living and to a right relationship with the Lord Himself. Our failure to do this will only contribute to the further downfall and, I believe, ultimate destruction of America as we have known it.

Spiritual warfare is at a high peak. We are witnessing firsthand that "we wrestle not against flesh and blood but against principalities, against powers, against the rulers of the darkness of this world, against spiritual wickedness in high places" (Ephesians 6:12). How we need to prayerfully plead for the help of our God to turn the tide of evil in our land and help us once again to be a "blessed nation where God is the Lord." Join me, if you will, in such a prayer as we find in Psalm 80:3, "Restore us, O God and cause your face to shine and we shall be saved."

The upcoming election, I believe, is perhaps the most important in my lifetime. There is so much at stake, including the probability of two Supreme Court justices being chosen in the near future. This alone will greatly impact our country and society for years to come. I pray that the Lord will answer our prayers in mercy and grace, giving us what we need and not what we deserve. Thankfully, our hope is not in any man or political party, but rather in the Lord God Almighty "who only does wondrous things."

Revival in our land seems so far away at present, but may we be reminded that "with God, all things are possible." How I personally long for that to take place before our Lord returns or calls me home. The psalmist prayed that the God of our salvation help us for the glory of his name, which we often pray perhaps selfishly for the sake of our families. Perhaps we would do well to join the psalmist in asking for revival to come for the glory of God. When it does come, it will be totally his doing, and all glory goes to him who loved us and washed us from our sins through his atoning death on the cross.

The Battle Is Raging

First Timothy 6:12 "Fight the good fight of faith, lay
hold on eternal life, unto which thou art also called."

As I write these words, I am keenly aware of and prayerfully concerned for our men and women in our armed forces who, at
this moment, are in harm's way, risking their lives for each of us here
in America. When we carefully examine the situation, we realize the
fight is much larger than Iraq or Afghanistan. Our troops are fighting
the physical battle to preserve our freedom and that of the Iraqis and
Afghan people, but from the spiritual side, what is at stake is our very
culture and the existence of Western civilization as we know it.

At the heart of the War on Terrorism is an ideology, a religious
lifestyle that extremists and radical Muslims want to impose upon
civilization as a whole. World conquest is their ultimate objective.
As believers in Christ, we must realize we are in spiritual warfare and
the head of the army of our enemy is none other than Satan himself.

Spiritual warfare began in the Garden of Eden where the old
serpent, the devil, sought to destroy every good thing God made,
including man. For all these thousands of years, his objective has
not changed though his physical army has; including those in our
lifetime, such as the Japanese, Germans, and Russians. Now it is
Al-Qaida, Hamas, Iran, North Korea, and the Islamic terrorists.
Jesus said of Satan, "The thief cometh not but to steal, and to kill
and to destroy" (John 10a). The truth of what we are witnessing is
clearly defined in Ephesians 6:12 "For we wrestle not against flesh
and blood, but against principalities, against powers; against rulers
of the darkness of this world, against spiritual wickedness in high

places." Like it or not, we are all affected by this spiritual warfare and need to be trained and well prepared for battle.

Our first order, as our text verse says, is for each of us to lay hold on eternal life to which we have been called. In other words, be sure you are a soldier of the cross. By God's grace, each of us who profess faith in Christ before many witnesses, have been called into the army of God through faith in the Lord Jesus Christ. John 15:16a "You have not chosen me, but I have chosen you, and ordained you, that you should go and bring forth fruit, and that your fruit should remain." Then we are encouraged in Second Peter 1:10, "Wherefore the rather, brethren, give diligence to make your calling and election sure; for if you do these things, you shall never fall." To properly and effectively engage in battle, we need to be equipped with the armor of God as outlined in Ephesians 6:11–18. As this is spiritual warfare, we need spiritual armor and preparation. Second Corinthians 10:4–5 "For the weapons of our warfare are not carnal, but mighty through God to the pulling down of strongholds. Casting down imaginations and every high thing that exalts itself against the knowledge of God, and bringing into captivity every thought to the obedience of Christ."

One of our most effective offensive weapons is the unlimited power of prayer. The great promise in the latter part of John 15:16 is "Whatsoever you shall ask the Father in my name, he may give it you." May the Lord help us to pray always as faithful warriors of God, remembering those on the physical battlefront as well as one another. Fight the good fight of faith, and remember, God will be victorious!

Abundance of Grace

Romans 5:17 "For if by the one man's offense death reigned through the one, much more those who receive abundance of grace and of the gift of righteousness will reign in life through the One, Jesus Christ."

The Bible teaches us a fundamental fact that sin entered the world through one man, Adam. As a result of his sin, death also entered into the world and spread to all men because all of us have sinned and fallen short of the glory of God. On the other hand, God's free gift of grace through the One, our Lord Jesus Christ, abounded to many. While the sin of Adam brought condemnation to all of us, the free gift of grace brought justification.

This gift is for those who are blessed to receive God's abundant and amazing grace. "For by grace you have been saved through faith and that not of yourselves; it is the gift of God, not of works, lest anyone should boast" (Ephesians 2:8–9). Please note in our text this grace is available to those who will receive it! The Bible says, "As many as received Him, to them He gave the right to become children of God, to those who believe in His name; who were born, not of blood, nor of the will of the flesh, nor of the will of man, but of God" (John 1:12 and 13).

This marvelous gift of grace, I believe, accomplishes far more than we realize. First, it brought us total and complete forgiveness for sins past, present, and future. Not only does God forgive our sin through Christ, but he forgets them! When the enemy attempts to remind us of past sins that have been confessed and forgiven, appropriate by faith these great promises: "I will forgive their iniquity, and their sin I will remember no more" (Jeremiah 31:34). The psalmist reminds us, "As far as the east is from the west, so far has He removed our transgressions from us" (Psalm 103:12). This is extravagant grace! Remember, our Heavenly Father views us through the soul-cleansing blood of the Lamb.

This abundant grace of God also gives us the gift of righteousness. When we receive the Lord Jesus into our hearts by faith, he transfers to our account his righteousness. Hear his Word "being justified freely by His grace through the redemption that is in Christ Jesus, whom God set forth as a propitiation by His blood, through faith, to demonstrate His righteousness ... that He might be just and the Justifier of the one who has faith in Jesus" (Romans 3:24–26). May this marvelous truth sink deep into our hearts and souls. Because of the atoning death of our Lord Jesus on Calvary, we are not only forgiven and cleansed but made righteous and justified freely by his grace. Though we are guilty and hell-deserving sinners, the Judge of all the earth, Almighty God, declares us "not guilty." Jesus took upon himself all of our sin and the penalty of our sin on the cross where he paid the price in full. It was there we were redeemed, bought back from the slavery of sin and death and set free by the grace and mercy of God.

Seasons of Life

Ecclesiastes 3:1 "To everything there is a season, and a time to every purpose under the heaven."

As a good friend once said, "Growing old is wonderful when we consider the options." This is certainly true for although we are spiritually prepared by God's amazing grace to be with him, we have within us the quality of self-preservation. Unless one is deathly ill, we all would like to enjoy a little more time with family and friends.

Those of us in our senior years can but wonder where the years have gone so quickly. The Bible reminds us, "As for man, his days are like grass; as a flower of the field, so he flourishes. For the wind passes over it, and it is gone; and the place thereof shall know it no more" (Psalm 103:15–16). We are keenly aware that age has an effect on our physical bodies. Those of us blessed with good health are still able to do most of what we have always done; it may just take a little longer.

Let me be quick to say that each of us needs to strive in the strength of the Lord to continue to serve Him as long as He gives us life and are able. You recall when Jesus was praying in the Garden, that he asked the disciples to watch and pray with him. Being physically exhausted, however, they all fell asleep. And Jesus replied, "The spirit indeed is willing, but the flesh is weak" (Matthew 26:41b). To me, one of the keys in life to living a productive life for the Lord is to keep our spirits willing always to be available to him, even though we may experience physical limitations in our latter years, especially. The Bible says, "If there be first a willing mind, it is accepted according to that which a man has, and not according to that which he has not (2 Corinthians 8:12).

One thing is for certain, whether young or old, the Lord is ever faithful to each of us who belong to him. He is our sure hope for time and eternity. "You are my hope, O Lord; you are my trust from my youth. By you have I been held up from the womb; you are He who took me out of my mother; my praise shall be continually of you" (Psalm 71:5–6). Wherever we find ourselves in the cycle of life, may we join our hearts in love for our Lord and each other, to serve him who alone is worthy of our best and our all. "Whatsoever your hand finds to do, do it with your might" (Ecclesiastes 9:10). I join the psalmist in a word of testimony. "I have been young, and now am old; yet have I not seen the righteous forsaken, nor His seed begging bread. He is ever merciful and lendeth and his seed is blessed" (Psalm 37:25–26).

Faith Grows

First John 3:20–21 "If our heart condemns us, God is greater than our heart, and knows all things. Beloved, if our heart condemns us not, then have we confidence toward God."

As we grow in grace, we find that our trust in the Lord also grows, and we are able to get beyond self- condemnation. We can remind ourselves that "He, who the Son has set free, is free indeed." The Lord Jesus does not want his children burdened down with sin or with care because he has given us so many wonderful promises to alleviate any anxiety, fear, or doubt.

An example he gives us is found in 1 John 3, verse 22, "Whatsoever we ask, we receive of him, because we keep his commandments, and do those things that are pleasing in his sight." I learned many years ago that the best commentary on the Bible is the Bible itself. Such is the case here, for the question arises, to which of the commandments is the scripture referring? Verse 23 tells us very clearly and simply that we are to believe in his Son, the Lord Jesus Christ, and to love one another. What happens when we obey the scripture? Our prayer request and/or burden will be answered, according to the promise in verse 22.

In chapter 5, verses 14 and 15, we find this confirmation, "This is the confidence that we have in him, that if we ask anything according to his will, he hears us. And if we know he hears us, whatever we ask, we know that we have the petitions that we desired of him." See how our faith grows, and so does our confidence in the Lord. Now, as the writer of Hebrews encourages us, "Let us therefore, come boldly to the throne of grace that we may obtain mercy and find grace to help in time of need" (Hebrews 4:16).

A word of caution here. This is not a business deal or a bargaining situation with God. We are not to be obedient in order to get what we want and attempt to oblige the Lord into repaying us for our obedience. What point is Apostle John making? The more you and I enter into a relationship with the Lord by living in obedience to his commands, the more our asking will be in accordance with his will.

He Is Able

Psalm 17:5 "Hold up my goings in thy
paths, that my footsteps slip not."

What a marvelous salvation we have in the Lord Jesus Christ. We are saved by grace through faith, but in addition, the Lord sustains us in our everyday walk. None of us is capable of living the Christian life in our own strength. It is utterly impossible. As the psalmist realized, the Lord is the One who holds us up and leads us in the path of righteousness. The key for us is to realize our utter dependence on him. All of us fail and fall at times in our walk with the Lord, but by his grace and mercy, he picks us up and puts us back on the right path. Psalm 37:23 and 24 "The steps of a good man are ordered by the Lord, and He delighteth in his way. Though he fall, he shall not be utterly cast down; for the Lord upholdeth him with his hand."

Because of human pride, many times we make the mistake of trying to please the Lord in our own strength. This only leads to failure regardless of how sincere we may be in our efforts. We ought to be trusting instead of trying. Only through the power of the Lord can we live a victorious life. Hear the admonition of God's Word.

Psalm 116:8 "Thou hast delivered my soul from death, mine eyes from tears and my feet from falling." The psalmist clearly acknowledges the Lord having kept him on the exact path. Sometimes in life we take the wrong fork in the road. It is the road that leads us out of the will of God for our lives, and the road becomes a very difficult one resulting in disappointment, sorrow, and regret. It is heartbreaking when one of God's children takes this erroneous path in life, but

God always places a detour sign when we are enticed to take the wrong way. He knows it will lead to our fall and failure. What direction are you taking today?

Wherever we are in life's journey, our gracious Lord is willing to forgive and restore us to fellowship with him if that is our need. He is in the business of doing just that. We serve a God of mercy and grace who really longs to fellowship with his children.

Jude 1:24–25 "Now unto Him that is able to keep you from falling and to present you faultless before the presence of His glory with exceeding joy, to the only wise God, our Savior, be glory and majesty, dominion and power, both now and evermore. Amen."

Divine Counsel

Psalm 33:11 "The counsel of the Lord standeth forever,
the thoughts of his heart to all generations."

There are times in life for all of us when we find ourselves in need of good counsel. Even as I write this "Word," some of us are seeking the perfect will of God in certain matters. It may be what seems a minor issue or one of great magnitude, which could impact not only our personal lives but our family and perhaps the lives of countless others. It can be very costly to make a careless decision, so we need the best and wisest counsel.

Our first inclination, quite often, is to seek the counsel of others. The Bible addresses this in Proverbs 11:14, "Where no counsel is, the people fail, but in the multitude of counselors there is safety." It can be of great help to obtain wise counsel from godly men or women concerning a particular matter. There is a danger, however, in that we should be very careful who we confide in for counsel. Remember, for example, the poor counsel Job received from some of his so-called friends. Why, even his wife said, "Do you still retain your integrity? Curse God and die." Then again, it can be dangerous to seek counsel from any ungodly person. Psalm 1:1a "Blessed is the man who walketh not in the counsel of the ungodly."

While we may seek counsel from godly friends, may I suggest we not act upon their recommendation without first bringing the matter to the Lord to be certain the action taken is within His perfect will. We do well to remember we must wait on the Lord for the certainty of our decision. This is not easy to do, but extremely important and necessary.

After being led out of Egypt by the mighty hand of God, Israel had a spiritual lapse and made the mistake of acting on their own without getting approval from God. Psalm 106:13 "They soon forgot his works; they waited not for his counsel." Most of the mistakes we make in life are made because we fail to wait upon the Lord to confirm his will in a particular matter.

The final word and actually the only word we can totally rely upon is the word we receive from the Lord. Listen to this magnificent promise, "Nevertheless, I am continually with thee; thou hast held me by my right hand. Thou shall guide me with thy counsel and afterward receive me in glory. Whom have I in heaven but thee? And there is none upon earth that I desire beside thee" (Psalm 73:23–25).

Whatever your need, prayer concern or desire of your heart, bring it to the Lord today in faith, with full assurance that as we prayerfully wait for his counsel, the answer will surely come in his time. It may not be what we want to hear, but be sure it will be what is best for us and others who may be involved.

Share His Love

Psalm 68:11 "The Lord gave the word; great was
the company of those who published it."

One of the main responsibilities of the people of God seems to be
greatly neglected in our churches today. I refer to the fact that
so few of us make any effort to share the Word of God with others
in need of Christ or even a brother or sister in Christ who have great
need of encouragement and hope. Our fast-paced society keeps us
so busy doing so many things, some of which may be good, but we
neglect to share our faith—one of the primary things every Christian
is commissioned to do (Matthew 28:19–20).

Churches today offer everything from aerobics to needlework
but fail to train people in sharing their faith in Christ with others.
On the other hand, where this training is offered, I feel very few
would have any genuine interest. The church at Ephesus, in the book
of Revelation, was a good church overall, doing many things in a
proper way, perhaps, but they left their first love. My fear is that
many of our churches today are in the same set of circumstances. It is
estimated that over ten thousand of our churches never reached one
single individual for the Lord last year! A staggering fact.

In recent weeks, the Holy Spirit has placed his hand of conviction on my own heart, showing me that I too have failed to be as
conscious in sharing my faith with the lost among family and friends.
Like the churches in Revelation, chapters 2 and 3, the call is to repentance. It was James who wrote, "To him that knoweth to do good
and doeth it not, to him it is sin" (James 4:17). When we know what
to do and fail to do it, we are simply without excuse. The solution

is quite simple; we need to return to our first love. Sometimes if we are not careful, we can get so caught up in doing the "work of the Lord" that we unintentionally neglect spending adequate time with the Lord himself.

Let me encourage each of us to go into a quiet place of prayer to seek the Lord. In his Holy Presence, our first love can be revived and our sin can be cleansed. Please read Isaiah 6:1–8 as it contains many helpful truths to encourage our hearts. In his experience, Isaiah saw the Lord high and lifted up. This caused Isaiah to see himself as he really was, as it should do for us. "Then said I, woe is me! For I am undone, because I am a man of unclean lips, and I dwell in the midst of a people of unclean lips; for mine eyes have seen the King, the Lord of hosts" (Isaiah 6:5). Can we not totally identify with the great prophet? Then comes the grace and mercy of God, for we see the seraphim taking a live coal off the altar. "And he laid it upon my mouth and said, Lo, this has touched thy lips and thine iniquity is taken away and thy sin purged" (Isaiah 6:7). Now cleansed from our sin and failures, we are ready, by God's grace to make public his Word.

I close with an appropriate quote from Oswald Chambers, "If we let the Spirit of God bring us face to face with God, we too shall hear something akin to what Isaiah heard, the still small voice of God; and in perfect freedom will say, 'Here am I; send me.'"

The Substance of Faith

Hebrews 11:1 "Now faith is the substance of things
hoped for, the evidence of things not seen."

Notice in this great definition from the Word of God concerning faith that it is substance; it is not an unfounded leap in the dark, nor a blind guess or taking a chance. Faith is substance. How can this be when it refers to things hoped for yet not seen? Reading the eleventh chapter of Hebrews, faith's hall of fame, you will find that the meaning of faith is substance.

Abraham was called, and he went out not knowing where he went. Sarah, past the age of childbearing, judged him faithful who had promised; Noah, being warned of God. Through this great chapter, one thing is evident in these faithful followers of God; they got a word from God and acted upon it. They believed God would perform what He said He would do. Their faith resulted in obedient action to the promise and commands of God. It was Phil Price of Campus Crusade who said, "We only really believe that which activates us."

Faith is essential to salvation and an effective walk with the Lord. Hebrews 11:6 says, "Without faith it is impossible to please God."

Hebrews 11:13 says, concerning these great heroes of faith, "These all died in faith, not having received the promises but having seen them afar off and were persuaded of them, and embraced them." There was great substance to their faith. With the eyes of faith, they saw the promise far off; they were persuaded, affirmed in their hearts by faith that Almighty God would keep his word, so much so that they embraced the promises. In many cases, they did not receive the fulfillment of the promise in their lifetime, but that did not negate their faith or the fulfillment of the promise. God always keeps his word. Heaven and earth shall pass away, but not one word of God will pass away, not one promise will remain unfulfilled.

What about your faith? Are you totally trusting the Lord to fulfill his promises to you? We are blessed with a treasure chest full of promises from the Lord in his Holy Word. Promises so abundant to meet every need in our lives today. Will you claim them by faith today to meet the need of your heart? Bring your burden or concern to the Lord today and ask him to give you a promise for that concern from his Word. He will not only respond with a promise, but if you will claim it by faith, he will fulfill it.

Forever Faithful

Hebrews 3:1–3 "Wherefore, holy brethren, partakers of the heavenly calling, consider the Apostle and High Priest of our profession, Christ Jesus, who was faithful to him that appointed him, as also Moses was faithful in all his house. For this man was counted worthy of more glory than Moses, inasmuch as he who has built the house has more honor than the house."

Our amazing Lord has so many glorious attributes, not the least of which is his faithfulness. It is nothing short of an incredible thing to me how a Holy God and Savior can be forever faithful to us, even when we may be unfaithful to him. As the psalmist said, "He has not dealt with us after our sins, nor rewarded us according to our iniquities. For as the heavens are high above the earth, so great is his mercy toward them that fear him" (Psalm 103:10–11). Our Lord's faithfulness to us is forever—eternal! What a glorious truth to cling to especially when the storms of life come our way with troubles and trials. We understand clearly what it means for one to be faithful, but I found that *Webster's* dictionary gives an excellent description, particularly as it pertains to the Lord.

Faithful. "Unswervingly devoted, trustworthy, loyal to one's promise." Does this not, at least in human expression, accurately describe our Lord? His faithfulness is from the eons of the ages. He has always been and will eternally be faithful. John the Baptist said of him, "Behold the Lamb of God, who takes away the sin of the world" (John 1:29). This Lamb of God was a "lamb" slain from the foundation of the world (Revelation 13:8).

Our Heavenly Father, in his foreknowledge, saw the plight of man, knowing he would sin and fall short of God's glory. Knowing man's only hope for restoration after the fall was for a redeemer to come and buy man back from the curse and penalty of sin. The Bible tells us, "When the fullness of time was come, God sent forth His Son, made of a woman, made under the law, to redeem them that were under the law, that we might receive the adoption of sons" (Galatians 4:4–5).

His mission was clear, "The Son of Man is come to seek and to save that which was lost" (Luke 19:10). Knowing what was ahead and the tremendous cost he would pay for us, he remained faithful and unswervingly committed to finish the work the Father sent him to do. Isaiah tells us, "He is despised and rejected of men, a man of sorrows and acquainted with grief, he has borne our griefs and carried our sorrows, he was wounded for our transgressions, he was bruised for our iniquities; the chastisement for our peace was upon him and with his stripes we are healed." Forever faithful! Paul writes in Philippians 2:7–8, "He took upon himself the form of a servant, and was made in the likeness of men; and being found in fashion as a man, he humbled himself and became obedient unto death, even the death of the cross." Faithful indeed.

A Word to the Church

Hebrews 3:7–12 "Wherefore, as the Holy Spirit says, today
if you will hear his voice, harden not your hearts, as in the
day of provocation in the day of trial in the wilderness, when
your fathers put me to the test, proved me and saw my works
forty years. Wherefore, I was grieved with that generation,
and said, they do always err in their heart and they have not
known my ways. So I swore in my wrath, they shall not enter
into my rest. Take heed, brethren, lest there be in any of you
an evil heart of unbelief, in departing from the living God."

The question of the day is, isn't it so obvious that Almighty God
is trying to get our undivided attention? Have we stopped to
consider the major catastrophes our nation has experienced in the
last decade? We have witnessed a horrible terrorist attack on our
country by those set to destroy us. In addition, hurricanes Katrina
and Ike have caused major devastation, loss of life, and billions of
dollars in economic loss. We have had forest fires of great magnitude,
loss of crops, earthquakes, and a major war that took precious lives,
left many maimed and scarred for life, costing billions of dollars.

Someone may ask, do you think God is causing these things
to happen? My answer to that is simply "I do not know." God is
sovereign! One thing is sure, while he may not have caused these
catastrophes, he has allowed them to happen. God's favorite name
is love, but spurned love can turn to wrath. God desires and expects
his people to walk in obedience to him; to keep and honor his Word.

In our text, we are reminded again of the failures of Israel,
causing God to be angry with them. So the Holy Spirit is prodding

us to remember and learn from the mistakes of his people in Old Testament times. (I encourage you to read Psalm 104 and see how God dealt with his wayward ones.) Are we the redeemed ones, the church of the living God, hearing the voice of his Holy Spirit today? He is calling us back to our Heavenly Father in repentance and faith and encourages us not to have an evil heart of unbelief and depart from the living God.

What a needful time we live in! The recent Supreme Court decision will have major consequences on each of us, our children, grandchildren, and great grandchildren. Are you hearing the voice of the Lord today? What is he saying to you? Be obedient to His call and respond in faith. May we find encouragement in the fact that "whom the Lord loves He chastens and scourges every son whom he receives" (Hebrews 12:6). The Bible also says in Psalms 94:12, "Blessed is the man whom you chasten, O Lord and teaches him out of thy law." The Lord is not calling us to pay attention and learn in order to punish us, but rather for our benefit to walk with him so we may have peace in our hearts in the midst of life's storms and rest in our spirits from the problems of life.

No earthly father enjoys having to discipline his children, but he does it out of love for them knowing the value of their learning obedience. It builds character, including self-discipline, responsibility, and integrity. How much more does our Heavenly Father chasten and correct us for our own good. Hebrews 12:11 "Now no chastening for the present time seems to be joyous, but grievous; nevertheless, afterwards it yields the peaceable fruit of righteousness unto them who are exercised by it."

Prayers and Promises

James 5:16b "The effectual, fervent prayer
of a righteous man avails much."

As I write this devotion, I believe and trust that millions of God's redeemed across this land are pleading with God to have mercy on us, to forgive our sin and to heal our land. We can be assured from the Word of God, our prayers can be effective and avail much. We qualify as righteous men and women, through saving faith in the Lord Jesus Christ, not by any righteousness of our own, for the best of us have none. "For he has made him who knew no sin, to be sin for us, that we might be made the righteousness of God in him" (2 Corinthians 5:21). The need for prayer for our nation has never been greater.

The Bible records the necessity of and the power in intercessory prayer. Read again the story of the marvelous way Abraham interceded with God on behalf of his nephew, Lot, who dwelt in Sodom, which God planned to destroy along with Gomorrah (Genesis 18:17–33). Abraham pleaded with God to spare the city; first, if there were fifty righteous in Sodom, all the way down to ten. God granted the request of Abraham by saying he would spare Sodom, even if there were but ten righteous people in the land. Of course, we know there were not ten, and God rained down fire and brimstone on the two cities and destroyed them. He did, however, in mercy, spare Lot, his wife and two daughters. As I read this story again, I could not but think, with much sorrow, how America is so infested with sin, like Sodom, and wondered how many righteous ones will it take to spare us. Only our Sovereign God knows for sure. Is it not our responsibility, however, to intercede for our country and for one another, praying for God's mercy?

Our prayers matter greatly. Consider Esther, the queen, who learned that because of wicked Haman, her people, the Jews, were going to be killed. Mordecai, who had raised her as his own daughter, asked her, "Who knows whether you have come to the Kingdom for such a time as this?" As queen, Esther was in a unique but uncertain place to help her people. Esther called upon her people to intercede for her for three days. Then she made a courageous statement. "So will I go in unto the King, which is not according to the law, and if I perish, I perish" (Esther 4:15). God heard and answered the prayers of his people.

Samson, after wasting much of his life with wine, women, and the world, was captured by the Philistines and had his eyes put out. He was mocked and ridiculed by his enemies, but the Bible indicates Samson called unto the Lord to remember him and give him back his strength once more to avenge himself. The Bible records there were about three thousand Philistines on the roof of the house where Samson was being taunted. Being guided to the two pillars supporting the house, God heard his prayer, and Samson brought down the structure, killing all of the people. In fact, the Bible records, "So the dead whom he slew at his death were more than they whom he slew in his life," (Judges 16:30). God does answer prayer!

Acts chapter 12 records the imprisonment of Peter, and we find these words in verse 5, "Peter therefore was kept in prison; but prayer was made without ceasing by the Church unto God for him." Peter was miraculously freed from prison by an angel of God. James reminds us how the prayers of Elijah were so effective that God shut out the rain upon the earth for three and one-half years until he prayed again, and God sent rain. We are reminded also that Elijah was a man subject to passions as we are.

May these few brief examples remind us that our prayers on behalf of our nation and one another can make a difference. Jeremiah 33:3 "Call unto me, and I will answer thee and show thee great and mighty things, which thou knowest not."

Spiritual and Practical Help

Second Timothy 2:19 "The foundation of God standeth sure, having this seal, the Lord knoweth them that are his and let everyone that names the name of Christ depart from iniquity."

Let us review instances from a few Old Testament Bible characters and try to learn from their experiences and mistakes. Today, let us look at Samson in Judges, chapter 16.

God promised Samson's parents—Zorah, his father, and Manoah, his mother—a son, for Manoah was barren. Here is the promise found in Judges 13:5, "For lo, thou shalt conceive and bear a son and no razor shall come on his head; for the child shall be a Nazarite unto God from the womb. And he shall begin to deliver Israel from the hand of the Philistines." Then in verses 24 and 25 of the same chapter, we learn of Samson's birth, how he grew, and how the Lord blessed him. A key fact is that at times he was moved by the Spirit of the Lord.

Samson had incredible physical strength and power, but a great moral weakness—the lust of the flesh! This is evident in chapter 16 of Judges when he goes in to a harlot, then falls in love with Delilah even though he is married to Timnah, a Philistine woman. Even his marriage was outside the will of his parents, who wanted him to marry an Israelite. His weakness in the flesh made Samson an easy target for the devil, who used Delilah and her seductive ways to discover the secret of Samson's great strength. Delilah's objective was to deliver Samson into the hands of the Philistines. Unfortunately, Samson was not walking in the spirit but rather in the flesh. As a result of his moral failure, Samson lost his greatest possession, the spirit of the

Lord, which was often evident in his life. While asleep in the lap of the seductress, Delilah, they shaved off Samson's hair, which was his source of strength from God. Delilah awakened Samson from sleep as she had many times by saying, "The Philistines are upon thee." Then the most tragic words are recorded in Judges 16:20b, "And he knew not that the Lord was departed from him." You know the rest of the story; his eyes were put out, he was bound with fetters, and his ultimate death was the result.

What lessons we can learn from this story! Sin has costly consequences. Christians often fail to believe this or even consider it, for I believe anyone who genuinely weighs the cost of sin will do everything in his or her power with God's help to avoid sin in their lives. Every single day, we have choices to make that will affect our lives, our families, and our effectiveness for Christ. We are encouraged greatly in God's Word. Romans 6:12 "Let not sin, therefore, reign in your mortal body, that you should obey it in its lusts." Unlike Samson, we are blessed in that the Holy Spirit resides in our hearts forever. We are encouraged then to "walk in the Spirit, and you shall not fulfill the lust of the flesh" (Galatians 5:16). May the Lord help us one and all to do just that.

Wasted Years

Psalm 90:12 "Teach us to number our days, that
we may apply our hearts unto wisdom."

Last Wednesday, as some of us were sitting and talking together in the bass section of our choir, another man came to join our group. He had just become a choir member as of last July and spoke up and said something about doubts he had as it related to his salvation. The assurance of salvation is one of my favorite biblical studies to share, so I offered to bring him scripture that he could read and later we could discuss. However, he quickly responded by saying that he does not have these doubts any longer. The doubts had come when he was away from the Lord. He shared that although his dad was a Baptist minister, he personally had been away from the Lord for thirty years. I thought how sad this was, considering that he was probably in his mid-fifties. That meant he had been out of God's will for perhaps more than half his life.

"What brought you back?" I asked. He told me he had developed some health issues and realized how fragile life really is. This reminded me of two verses from Psalm 119. In verse 67, it reads, "Before I was afflicted, I went astray, but now have I kept thy word." In verse 71, it reads, "It is good for me that I have been afflicted, that I might learn your statues." God is a gracious and forgiving God, as evidenced by this man's life. He is very faithful now and active in our church and in our choir and is used on occasion on the platform with three others from different sections of choir.

While this is possible, because of God's amazing grace, I still find it quite sad when I think of the thirty years he wasted. Sad because those years can never be relived or brought back. They are lost for time and eternity. He will never know what the Lord wanted to accomplish through him during those lost years.

This dictates to me how important and undeniably true it is for each of us to remain close to the Lord regardless of age and where we are in life. Allow me to encourage those of you who are young believers, to be faithful to the Lord with your life. Build yourself up in the faith and be protective of your testimony and your walk with Christ. When you are my age, you will look back with a grateful heart to the Lord for his "keeping power." "Unto him that is able to keep you from falling, and to present you faultless before the presence of his glory with exceeding joy, to the only wise God, our Savior, be glory and majesty, dominion and power, both now and ever" (Jude 24–25).

Like my friend in the choir, if you find yourself away from the Lord, I urge you to come home to him in repentance and faith. I am reminded of that great old hymn, "Lord, I'm Coming Home." "I wasted many precious years, now I'm coming home. I now repent with bitter tears, Lord, I'm coming home." Jesus said, "Him that cometh to me I will in no wise cast out" (John 6:37b). While we will fail our Lord at times, I believe the closer we stay to him, yielded and obedient, the less likely we are to be lured away by the world, the flesh, and the devil. May our prayer be, "Teach me, O Lord, the way of your statutes and I shall keep it unto the end" (Psalm 119:33).

Working Out Our Salvation

Romans 13:11–12 "And that knowing the time, that now it is high time to awake out of sleep, for now is our salvation nearer than when we believed. The night is far spent, the day is at hand; let us, therefore, cast off the works of darkness and let us put on the armor of light."

This passage is so fresh and vibrant it is as if the Holy Spirit is sending this word from Heaven to the Church today via special delivery. Please note the urgency in the message. "It is high time to awake out of sleep"! What an appropriate word for us today when so many saints are virtually asleep spiritually while our country and society are on its way to destruction as a result of our individual and national sin and apathy! Paul seems to use this figure of speech, perhaps depicting a Roman soldier who awakes from a night of sleep, removes his sleeping garments and puts on his gleaming armor, ready to meet the challenges of the day.

As Christians, the implication to each of us is to cast off any besetting sin in our lives, including worldly habits, which belongs to unbelieving mankind and the kingdom of darkness. By contrast, we are to "put on" the whole armor of God that we may be able to stand against the wiles of the devil" (Ephesians 6:11).

The emphasis is in the statement, "Now is our salvation nearer than when we believed." I might add, than when we first believed. This passage is a stark reminder that our Lord Jesus Christ could return at any moment to rapture the Church and consummate our salvation.

Our salvation in Christ has three different phases, which we pass through on our way to its completion. They are the penalty of sin, which we have already been saved from; the power of sin, we are being saved from; and the presence of sin, which we ultimately will be saved from. Another example of this is found in the terms *justification*, *sanctification*, and *glorification*. When we are born again through faith in Christ, we become a new creation in him. "If any man be in Christ, he is a new creation, old things pass away, behold all things become new" (2 Corinthians 5:17). Although at the time of our new birth we understand only that we have been redeemed, in reality, our salvation is complete.

The Bible reminds us, "For in him dwells all the fullness of the Godhead bodily. And you are complete in him who is the head of all principality and power" (Colossians 2:9–10). In light of all the heresy that abounds today, it is crucial to understand this. The Holy Spirit is given to us at our new birth to empower us, to teach and guide us so that we can work out our salvation for the glory of God!

Seek the Lord

Lamentations 3:24–25 "The Lord is my portion says my soul; therefore will I hope in Him. The Lord is good to those who wait for Him, to the soul that seeks Him."

One thing we can be sure of today, as our scripture says, our hope for today, as well as the future, is in the Lord. It is vital now more than ever that each of us whose faith is in the risen Lord Jesus Christ, that we seek his forgiveness, presence, and guidance with our whole heart in our daily lives. Anyone who genuinely desires to live for Christ and make a difference with their lives within the family circle and among friends will be in a minority.

Look for Christians to endure more and more criticism, and ultimately, I believe, even persecution from the world. Jesus said, "Remember the word that I said to you, the servant is not greater than his lord [or master]. If they have persecuted me, they will also persecute you; if they have kept My saying, they will keep yours also. All these things will they do to you for My name's sake, because they know not Him that sent Me" (John 15:20–21).

We can take comfort, however, in the words of our Lord; "These things I have spoken unto you, that in Me you might have peace. In the world you shall have tribulation; but be of good cheer, I have overcome the world" (John 16:33). Well do I realize that these words originally were given to the disciples, but rest assured, they do and will apply to all who will seek to live a godly life. God is good to us even when we are totally undeserving of his goodness. "It is because of the Lord's mercies that we are not consumed because His compassions fail not. They are new every morning; great is your faithfulness"

(Lamentations 3:22–23). This is especially true to all who make a sincere effort to seek him!

The invitation is to all, "Seek the Lord while He may be found, call you upon Him while He is near; Let the wicked forsake his way and the unrighteous man his thoughts and let him return unto the Lord and He will have mercy upon him and to our God; for He will abundantly pardon" (Isaiah 55:6–7).

These verses further confirm that the mercies of the Lord are new every morning and that his faithfulness is great! My soul cries within me, "How great thou art, how great thou art!"

Needless Worry

Matthew 6:25 "Therefore I say to you, do not worry
about your life, what you will eat or what you will drink;
nor about your body what you will put on. Is not life
more than food and the body more than clothes?"

How many of us worry, spend time being anxious about the basic necessities of life? No one knows us like the Lord, who looks on the heart of man, so he addresses one of our weaknesses in verse 25. Speaking to the Jews, he also says, "After all these things the Gentiles seek." Keep in mind at this point in time the Gospel was not yet preached to Gentiles openly. Relatively few were believers. Of all people who should trust God for provision, it was Israel. Psalms 105–107 address some of Israel's history and the miraculous way God provided even in the wilderness.

We know, however, though originally this Word was given to the Jews, it equally applies to us today. In order to fully understand what the Lord is saying, let us first consider what he is not saying. In no way does this scripture imply we should just sit back and wait on God to provide our needs while we do nothing. Common sense, as well as scripture, indicates otherwise. "If anyone will not work, neither shall he eat" (2 Thessalonians 3:10). "We urge you, brethren, that you increase more and more; that you also aspire to lead a quiet life, to mind your own business, and to work with your own hands" (1 Thessalonians 4:10–11).

Regarding the caring and providing for our families, the scripture reminds us, "If anyone does not provide for his own, and especially for those of his household, he has denied the faith and is worse than an unbeliever" (1 Timothy 5:8). This truth is further confirmed in Ephesians 5:28–29, "Husbands ought to love their own wives as their own bodies; he who loves his wife loves himself. For no one ever hated his own flesh, but nourishes it, just as the Lord does the church." Obviously then, we are to concern ourselves with the responsibility of providing food, shelter, and clothing for our loved ones as well as ourselves, but concern and worry are two different things.

May I suggest the next time you are tempted to worry about tomorrow, take time to be quiet before the Lord and remember how he has always faithfully provided for you and me over the years. As the scripture says, "I have been young, and now am old; yet I have not seen the righteous forsaken, nor his descendants begging bread," (Psalm 37:25). God is always faithful to his children and will never leave us or forsake us at any time.

While fulfilling our responsibilities as men, husbands, and fathers, we are to walk by faith and perform our work as unto the Lord. "Whatever you do in word or deed, do all in the name of the Lord Jesus giving thanks to God the Father through Him" (Colossians 3:17). Let's not allow worry to cause us to fear. Worry and fear will only hinder our walk with the Lord. We work as though everything we do depends on us, knowing it all depends on him and his marvelous provision. Most of us have probably experienced difficult times, and perhaps some are going through such times now. With all of the uncertainty, it would be easy to worry. Let's remind ourselves, "The just shall live by faith" (Romans 1:17). In good times or bad, may we be reminded, "My God shall supply all your need according to His riches in glory by Christ Jesus" (Philippians 4:19).

A Lion Is Loose

First Peter 5:8 "Be sober, be vigilant, because your
adversary, the Devil, like a roaring lion walks
about, seeking whom he may devour."

Scripture gives us a stern warning that the devil, our adversary, is on the loose seeking whom he may devour. It is no accident that the Holy Spirit here uses the metaphor *lion* for the Bible says, "A lion which is strongest among beasts, and turns not away for any" (Proverbs 30:30). We would make a huge mistake to underestimate the power of the wicked one; that is why we are encouraged to be sober (serious) and vigilant. Christians should constantly and consistently be alert for an attack from Satan. The moment we allow our guard to be inoperative, even for a moment, like a lion, he will pounce upon us. Remember also that he is a deceiver and will attack when we least expect it and sometimes through means that seem so innocent.

Satan is also a master of disguise. Remember how he disguised himself in the Garden of Eden. He is subtle and deceptive. The Bible further alerts us to his deceptive methods. "Satan himself is transformed into an angel of light. Therefore, it is no great thing if his ministers also be transformed as the ministers of righteousness" (2 Corinthians 11:14–15).

Just because someone stands with a Bible in his or her hand, do not take it for granted that they are teaching truth. For this reason, the scripture encourages us. "Beloved, believe not every spirit, but test the spirits whether they are of God; because many false prophets are gone out into the world" (1 John 4:1). Satan has his angels and false prophets everywhere. Their mission is to deceive and blind men and women from hearing and understanding truth. "If our gospel be hidden it is hidden to them that are lost, in whom the God of this age has blinded the minds of them who believe not, lest the light of the glorious gospel of Christ, who is the image of God, should shine unto them" While Satan cannot blind the children of God who have taken refuge in Christ for salvation, he uses every means available to him to mislead, deceive, and initiate doubt and destruction. Thank God his power against us is limited. "For there shall arise false Christs, false prophets, and shall show great signs and wonders, insomuch that, if it were possible, they shall deceive the very elect" (Matthew 24:24). Through the power of the Holy Spirit abiding in us, it is not possible for the elect to be deceived, but we need to be diligent in the study of God's Word and in prayer for our families and for one another.

Sure Hope

Proverbs 28:13 "He that covereth his sins shall not prosper, but whoever confesses and forsakes them shall have mercy."

As long as Almighty God chastens us when we fail to obey him, there remains hope for us individually and as a nation. In this time of national crisis, created primarily by self-serving, corrupt individuals, I believe God is calling you and me to repentance, confession, and the forsaking of our sinful ways. Can we not see ourselves before a Holy God as Isaiah did when he cried, "Woe is me! For I am undone, because I am a man of unclean lips and I dwell in the midst of a people of unclean lips; for mine eyes have seen the King, the Lord of hosts" (Isaiah 6:5).

As Christians, we have a choice. To ignore God could result in his saying to us as he said to Ephraim, "Ephraim is joined to idols, let him alone" (Hosea 4:17). It is my personal belief, at this time in the history of America, the response of God's people to the call for repentance will determine the future of our nation for generations to come. May each of us, by the grace of God through the power of his Holy Spirit, say with Joshua today, "Choose you this day whom you will serve … as for me and my house, we will serve the Lord" (Joshua 24:15). We can then claim the promise, "If we confess our sins, he is faithful and just to forgive us our sins, and to cleanse us from all unrighteousness" (1 John 1:9). For the sake of our children, grandchildren, great-grandchildren, and this nation we love, how can we do any less?

When we have our hearts right with God and one another, the possibilities through prayer are immeasurable. Let us consider some great promises from God's Holy Word. "Call unto me, and I will answer you, and show you great and mighty things; which you know not" (Jeremiah 33:3). Christian friend, are you anxious and fearful for the future? Are you overly concerned about the troubled waters our nation is in? Are the flames burning away the soul of our country causing you to be depressed? There is a word of hope. "Fear not; for I have redeemed you, I have called you by your name; you are mine. When you pass through the waters, I will be with you. When you walk through the fire, you shall not be burned, neither shall the flame kindle upon you. For I am the Lord your God, the Holy One of Israel, your Savior" (Isaiah 43:1–3).

May I encourage us one and all to look to the Lord. He knows us by name, promised never to leave us, redeemed us with his own precious blood, keeps us through the power of his Holy Spirit, coming again as King of Kings and Lord of Lords to claim his chosen bride, the Church. "My hope is built on nothing less, than Jesus, blood, and righteousness. I dare not trust the sweetest frame but wholly lean on Jesus's name. On Christ the solid Rock I stand, all other ground is sinking sand. All other ground is sinking sand!"

Remembering His Overwhelming Resources

Ephesians 1:3, "Blessed be the God and Father of
our Lord Jesus Christ, who has blessed us with all
spiritual blessings in heavenly places in Christ."

Remember growing up when your friends wanted to play baseball
or football and when sides were picked, you always hoped someone would pick you and preferably early on? None of us ever wanted
to be left out. It was and still is important to be accepted and loved
by family and friends. In my generation, there was no such thing as
peer pressure, at least not to me. Perhaps it was because I had and
still have no desire to associate with the elite or people of celebrity
status. Being a most ordinary individual, I thoroughly enjoy having
fellowship with those who are *real*, with no desire to impress by status
in life, or with many possessions to their name. Kathy and I feel very
blessed to have a multitude of friends who love us and accept us with
all our faults, blunders, and slipups.

Have you ever felt left out or rejected? The Bible has good
news for you. Try to grasp the great truth found in Ephesians 1:4,
"According as He has chosen us in Him before the foundation of
the world, that we should be holy and without blame before Him
in love." Think of it! God loves you and me and chose us in Christ
Jesus even before he ever made the world. Is that not amazing grace!
In addition to being chosen, look at Ephesians 1:6, "To the praises
of the glory of His grace through which He has made us accepted in
the Beloved." Chosen and accepted! These two truths should lift the

heart and soul of anyone having experienced rejection of any kind. Think of it, the God of the universe, Creator of all that is, loves you and me so much that he chose us, saved us by his amazing grace; and through the sacrifice of Christ on the cross, he has made us accepted in the Beloved.

We find even greater clarification of what the Lord did for us in Colossians 1:19–22. "For it pleased the Father that in Him [Jesus] should all fullness dwell. And, having made peace through the blood of His cross, by Him to reconcile all things unto Himself by Him, I say, whether they be things in earth or things in Heaven, and you that were once alienated and enemies in your mind by wicked works, yet now has He reconciled. In the body of His flesh through death to present you holy and unblamable and unreprovable in His sight." The work of reconciliation brought us into a right relationship with Christ. We are chosen in him, reconciled to God through his sacrifice, and accepted in the Beloved. Remember all of his benefits and resources, and offer to him worship and praise for he alone is worthy.

Broken Relationships

Matthew 5:23–24 "Therefore, if you bring your gift to the altar and there remember that your brother has anything against you, leave there your gift before the altar and go your way; first be reconciled to your brother and then come and offer your gift."

T he word *therefore* refers back to verses 21 and 22 of this chapter. Spoken in the midst of the Sermon on the Mount, Jesus is emphasizing how serious it is to be angry with a brother (or sister) without cause, or to have ill will or contempt toward a brother, and finally, the most serious of anger expressing itself in open rebuke of a brother. These three expressions of evil show a progression of punishment growing more severe each time. In fact, the Lord equates the severest sin of anger with murder.

As we ponder the full meaning of these verses, several things come to mind. The first thing apparent to me is that we are not prepared to worship our Lord when we knowingly have wronged another and made no effort to ask forgiveness. In such a case, one should first confess his or her sin to the Lord, then ask forgiveness of the one they have wronged. In some cases, a problem can exist in a relationship, destroying fellowship between parties, with one of the parties not even aware as to why the relationship is shattered or destroyed. Despite any attempt to find reconciliation, it cannot succeed unless both parties really want to be reconciled. This, to me, is very sad indeed, but we hear of these things happening with families, individuals, and even in church fellowships. In such cases, everyone involved suffers the consequences. Sometimes unrestored relationships go on for years, unresolved, and precious time between those involved is lost forever.

One of my favorite stories of reconciliation is that of Jacob and Esau. After Esau sold his birthright to Jacob for a bowl of porridge, Jacob, with help from his mother, deceived the aging Isaac, his father, into giving the blessing to him, though it should have been Esau's blessing. As a result, Esau hated Jacob, so Jacob fled for his life. Many years of broken relationship went by until, finally, the two came face-to-face as recorded in Genesis, chapter 33. Jacob feared greatly what Esau may do to him, but the Bible records when Esau saw Jacob afar off, "Esau ran to meet him and embraced him and fell on his neck and kissed him; and they wept" (Genesis 33:4). What a beautiful picture of forgiveness and reconciliation.

The answer to all broken relationships, in my opinion, is found in 1 Corinthians, chapter 13. This great chapter of Christian love for one another is highlighted in verses 4 through 8 where we find the crowning thought, "Love never fails." It never fails in marriages, in families, or in church fellowships when practiced scripturally. John the Beloved Disciple wrote in 1 John 3:14, "We know we have passed from death unto life because we love the brethren." It was our Lord Jesus who said, "This is my commandment that you love one another as I have loved you" (John 15:12). Think about how he loved us. He gave his all on Calvary's cross to redeem us from sin and reconcile us to God. Not only is Jesus a great example of love, but his love is the greatest of all. For in his own words, he said, "Greater love has no man than this, that a man lay down his life for his friends. You are my friends, if you do whatever I command you" (John 15: 13–14).

Bound

Mark 3:27 "No one can enter a strong man's house
and plunder his goods, unless he first binds the strong
man. And then he will plunder his house."

It appears to me, through his subtle and deceptive practices, Satan is plundering our country. As previously stated, he is stealing the souls of men; viciously attacking believers and using every means at his disposal to destroy America. Why is this happening? I believe it is within the permissive will of God who is calling us to repentance. "Your own wickedness will correct you, and your backslidings will rebuke you. Know therefore and see that it is an evil and bitter thing that you have forsaken the Lord your God, and the fear of me is not in you says the Lord God of hosts" (Jeremiah 2:19).

Although a strong nation militarily, we are bound by Satan as a result of our moral decay, sin, and disobedience to God, and therefore weak and dependent. Is it not time to "awake to righteousness and do not sin; for some do not have the knowledge of God. I speak this to your shame" (1 Corinthians 15:34). "Therefore he says: awake, you who sleep, arise from the dead, and Christ will give you light" (Ephesians 5:14). Our strength is not in our military might but in the Lord God who alone is our fortress, our shield, our defender, our hope, and our Eternal King!

Ironically for Americans, some of the great liberties and free-doms won for us by our founding fathers are being used against us. In the name of political correctness and tolerance, we are self-destruct-ing. Consider the following. God said, "Thou shall not kill." Yet our government has legalized abortion. Appealing to hellish pride, Satan has convinced millions that a woman's body is her own and it is okay to abort an unwanted child.

God said, "Thou shall not commit adultery." This commandment is ignored by countless numbers in our society who live a permissive lifestyle, believing they can live as they please with no thought of judgment. The lust of the flesh and the eyes enslave many to pornography, illicit sex, and adultery.

God further said, "Thou shall not covet." Many states have approved the lottery under the guise of using the money to help schools, appealing to the covetousness of men who hope to strike it rich.

God said, "Thou shall have no other gods before me." America, built on Judaeo-Christian principals, is no longer the same Christian nation. We have allowed mosques, other places of worship, and many other false gods into our country brought to America by those who are not believers, worshipping under the guise of religious freedom. I do not believe that this is what our founding fathers intended when they desired religious freedom for all, and I know our Heavenly Father is not pleased that we are shutting him out of America.

"Blessed is the nation whose God is the Lord" (Psalm 33:12).

Responding to God's Holiness

Isaiah 6:8 "I heard the voice of the Lord saying: Whom shall I send, and who will go for us? Then I said, 'Here am I! Send me.'"

As we study this passage, we learn that Isaiah went through four stages, and it is important for us to realize that we too must pass through these stages because we will experience some of these same things if we are to be used of God. In recent weeks, we saw Isaiah first encountered God in all of his majesty and glory, and he became conscious of his awesome presence. Isaiah recognized his own sinful condition, resulting in confession of his sin and unworthiness. Then as a result of God's grace, Isaiah experienced the cleansing of his sin.

The next phase of Isaiah's knowledge and understanding was the calling of God. I do not believe that you and I will ever find and accomplish God's perfect plan for our lives unless and until we, like Isaiah, experience what he did. God is not going to use a soiled vessel. Our hearts and our lives need to be clean and available to him for his use. Years ago after preaching in a small country church, a gentleman shook hands with the young preacher after services and said, "Son, God will use you if you remain usable." I have never forgotten that moment.

It is my belief that today, in the midst of a chaotic world, God is still calling out men and women to live separated lives, to share the Gospel and make a difference whenever and however we can. We are encouraged in God's Word with this, "I beseech you therefore, brethren, by the mercies of God, that you present your bodies a living sacrifice, holy, acceptable to God, which is your reasonable service. And do not be conformed to this world, but be transformed by the renewing of your mind, that you may prove what is that good and acceptable and perfect will of God" (Romans 12:1).

If ever there was a time that our world, and especially our nation, needed light and salt, it is *now!* Millions of professing Christians are conforming to this sinful world to the extent that in many churches across the nation, there is *no* light and *no* salt. Believers are losing influence daily because we have compromised whatever convictions we may have had. The preaching of the Gospel is so watered down we seldom hear sermons calling out congregations to repentance of sin. Everything that is happening right before our eyes is evidence that we are living in the Last Days, and time is very short before the Lord comes again. Signs of the times are everywhere. This passage in 2 Timothy 4:2–4 is so applicable, "Preach the word! Be ready in season and out of season. Convince, rebuke, exhort with all long suffering and teaching. For the time will come when they will not endure sound doctrine, but according to Their own desires, because they have itching ears, they will heap up for themselves teachers, and they will turn their ears away from the truth and be turned aside to fables." That time is *now!*

A Grave Responsibility

Deuteronomy 11:18–19 "Therefore shall you lay up these my words in your heart and in your soul and bind them for a sign upon your hand, that they may be as frontlets between your eyes. And you shall teach them to your children, speaking of them when thou walkest by the way, when thou liest down and when thou risest up."

The scripture is quite clear how important it is for each of us to saturate our hearts and soul with the Word of God. This, in my opinion, is the only way we can possibly live the overcoming life for our Lord and Savior in the midst of a sinful world with a society that is deteriorating more every day. This is not only crucial for our well-being, but for the good of our children and grandchildren. It is a sad truth today that many professing Christians know so little about the Word of God and seem to have no interest in studying to equip themselves and their families for life and godly living. Is not this one of the primary reasons that we are losing our children and grandchildren to the world? So many are growing up in homes where Christ is not the head of the home, so they have no interest in the things of God, including attending church.

It has long been my personal conviction that the major responsibility for our children and grandchildren learning to know and love the Lord, falls primarily on the shoulders of every dad and granddad. Now thank God for godly wives, mothers, and grandmothers who are usually the glue that holds a family together. Their love, care, and concern is so important, but men are to be the spiritual leaders in the home and set the example for the family.

Our text verse confirms the significance of laying up God's Word in our hearts as does hundreds of other verses, such as Psalm 119:11, "Thy word have I hidden in my heart, that I might not sin against thee." Then in Psalm 119:9, "Wherewithal shall a young man cleanse his way? By taking heed thereto according to the word." This should only be a starting place for each of us, however, because our responsibility to the Lord is much greater.

Please read our text verse again. The Lord is showing us that he is interested in lifestyle stewardship. This means he is the central One in our lives, affecting how we live, work, and serve him. Seeking the Lord first and his purpose is what we should be all about. In addition, we are to daily share the great truths of God's Word with our children and grandchildren. It is virtually from morning to evening. Let me encourage each of us, if this is not your lifestyle, it is not too late to begin. God is a God of love and forgiveness who greatly desires his children to walk with him.

I encourage you to read the eleventh chapter of Deuteronomy to see how the Lord is instructing Israel and us through his Word. The Lord says, "I speak not with your children who have not known and who have not seen the chastisement of the Lord your God. But your eyes have seen all the great acts of the Lord which He did," (Deuteronomy 11:2a and 7). We owe it to the Lord and to our families to share his greatness and love.

The Offering of Isaac

Genesis 22:1–2 "And it came to pass after these things, that
God did test Abraham, and he said unto him, Abraham:
And he said, Behold, here I am. And he said, Take now thy
son, thine only son Isaac, whom thou lovest, and get thee
into the land of Moriah; and offer him there for a burnt
offering upon one of the mountains which I tell thee of."

Initially, this must have seemed a very perplexing and foreign
request coming from God to Abraham. After the miraculous birth
of Isaac to Abraham and Sarah, and the promise that through this son
of promise God would bless not only Abraham, but all the nations of
the world, the Lord now commands that Abraham sacrifice Isaac to
him. Has God ever commanded you to do something that, humanly
speaking, did not seem to make sense? As with Abraham, this can be
a tremendous test of our faith. In reading and studying this passage,
I find it very difficult to put myself in Abraham's place. I cannot even
imagine how he must have felt.

Abraham has now walked with God for many years, and
although he has failed in his faith at times, he knows that God has
never failed him. I see Abraham as greatly matured with a faith in
God that is strong and secure. When God first commanded Abraham
to leave all and follow him, Abraham, in childlike faith, obeyed
(Genesis 12:1–4). Once again, we find Abraham is ready to obey the
Lord God's command, even though this one had to be very difficult.
I believe there is a distinct difference in what transpired this time,
however. The first time the Bible records, "By faith Abraham, when
he was called to go out into a place which he should after receive

for an inheritance, obeyed; and he went out, not knowing where he went" (Hebrews 11:8).

This time, based on scripture, which we shall review, I believe upon receiving the command to offer up Isaac, Abraham was on his face before God, desiring a word from the Lord; and through the eyes of faith, Abraham trusted God and saw the outcome. Please read this great story as recorded in Genesis 22:1–14.

After journeying three days by donkey with Isaac, his son, and two of his young men who carried wood for the burnt offering, Abraham sees the place where he is to go, afar off. Do not miss the great statement of faith that occurs at this time. "And Abraham said unto his young men, abide you here with the ass; and I and the lad will go yonder and worship, and come again to you" (Genesis 22:5). Abraham was positive, even if he had to slay Isaac on the altar of sacrifice, that God would raise him up. This is confirmed in scripture. Hebrews 11:17–19 "By faith Abraham, when he was tested, offered up Isaac; and he that had received the promises offered up his only begotten son, Of whom it was said, In Isaac shall thy seed be called; Accounting that God was able to raise him up, even from the dead, from which also he received him in a figure."

What great lessons for us in this story! The God of the impossible does not ask us to do anything that he will not equip us through his Holy Spirit to accomplish. Like Abraham, may we learn to trust God in all circumstances for he is wholly trustworthy and forever faithful!

Debt Crisis—Solved!

John 8:32 "You shall know the truth,
and the truth shall make you free."

While Congress and the White House continue to hassle over our nation's massive debt, how thankful every believer should be that the greater debt, our sin debt, has been paid in full by our Lord Jesus Christ. The scripture tells us that "All have sinned and come short of the glory of God" (Romans 3:23). Furthermore, "The wages of sin is death" (Romans 6:23). Each and every one of us, accountable for our own sin, accumulated a huge debt, which we are totally unable to pay.

What an amazing act of grace that "God commended His love toward us in that while we were yet sinners, Christ died for us" (Romans 5:8). Indeed, our Heavenly Father "has made Him, who knew no sin, to be sin for us, that we might be made the righteousness of God in Him" (2 Corinthians 5:21).

Unlike Washington, God, the Father, had a plan to completely erase our debt. In his foreknowledge, he saw, before the world was created, the fall of Adam, which would plunge the entire human race into sin, accumulating a debt that man was, by any means of his own, unable to pay. God's plan needed no amendments; it was irrevocable and guaranteed to all who would believe and receive by faith his free gift of forgiveness.

The Bible tells us that "God so loved the world that He gave His only begotten Son, that whosoever believeth on Him should not perish, but have everlasting life" (John 3:16). For "As many as received

Him, to them gave He power to become the children of God, even to them that believe on His name" (John 1:12).

There is absolutely no other plan that can wipe away our sin debt. Religion, good works, keeping the law, or any other idea man may have. The Bible is clear. "Neither is there salvation in any other, for there is no other name under Heaven given among men, whereby we must be saved" (Acts 4:12). Jesus went to the cross, fulfilled the law's demands, paid with his own precious blood for our sins, and is able to save to the uttermost all who come to God by him.

His sacrifice on Calvary was necessary for our redemption; it was complete! As he finished the work of atonement on the cross, the Father was pleased and accepted the sacrifice of his Son. "He shall see of the travail of His soul, and shall be satisfied; by His knowledge shall my righteous servant justify many; for he shall bear their iniquities" (Isaiah 53:11).

What are the results of God's plan? "The work of righteousness shall be peace; and the effect of righteousness, quietness and assurance forever" (Isaiah 32:17). Further proof of the results of our Lord's atonement was in his resurrection from the dead! "This man, after He had offered one sacrifice for sins forever, sat down on the right hand of God" (Hebrews 10:12).

It is finished! Our sin debt has been paid!

The Greatest Gift

1 Corinthians 13:13 "And now abide faith, hope, love,
these three; but the greatest of these is love."

The thirteenth chapter of 1 Corinthians is a great chapter from God's Holy Word that deals with the indispensable gift of love. Inspired by the Holy Spirit, the letter was written by Apostle Paul to the troubled church in Corinth. Not only was the church involved in flagrant immorality, but in need of knowing and practicing sound doctrine. At one point, Apostle Paul referred to them as babes feeding on the milk of God's Word when, as physically mature adults, they should have been feasting on the meat of God's Word. A study of First and Second Corinthians reveals the massive problems they encountered. It is not my desire at this time, however, to revisit the sin and error of the Corinthian congregation, but rather to study this chapter and apply its great truths to our lives.

It is my firm conviction that the eternal truths revealed in this marvelous chapter, when received in our hearts and experienced in our lifestyle, will transform, not only our lives, but will impact our family, church fellowship, business associates, and friends. It can do no less!

There is much talk today on the subject of love and contrasting views on how it is defined. Interestingly enough, however, as we study this chapter, we see that Paul does not attempt to define, describe, or even analyze love, but instead, he prefers to see love in action. Not only do we see what love does, but we also see what it does not do. In the context of this study, it is immediately obvious that the love addressed here transcends human love. The reference unquestionably depicts agape love. This love can only be experienced and expressed by those having been born again through saving faith in the Lord Jesus Christ. While this love is difficult to define, it is quite easy to discern, both in the life of our Lord and in those, his children, who walk in this love.

In setting the foundation for this study, please allow me to ask a few questions. What is the greatest desire of your heart? If you had but one gift, what would be the ultimate gift you desired? In your mind, what is the supreme good? Each of us has but one life to live, which, at best, is fleeting rapidly. The scripture has much to say about God-love. In fact, we could not cover it all in a lifetime. The beloved Apostle John tells us, "God is love" (1 John 4:8). Peter writes concerning the significance of love this way, "Above all things have fervent love for one another" (1 Peter 4:8). I would like to issue a challenge to each of you to join me in devoting time weekly to read the thirteenth chapter of 1 Corinthians a minimum of once weekly. It will make a difference as we experience firsthand the confirmation that the greatest gift is love. I close with a familiar rule of life, "I shall pass through this world but once. Any good thing, therefore, that I can do, or any kindness that I can show to any human being, let me do it now. Let me not defer it, or neglect it, for I shall not pass this way again." Only one life, so soon it will pass, only what is done for Christ will last!

Will You Watch?

Matthew 26:40—41 "And He cometh unto the disciples, and findeth them asleep; and He saith unto Peter, What, could you not watch with me one hour? Watch and pray, that you enter not into temptation; the spirit indeed is willing, but the flesh is weak."

The scene of our first text is the Garden of Gethsemane. For our Lord Jesus, it is a trying and most difficult time. Along with his disciples, he has just celebrated the last Passover in which he would partake while on earth. We would do well to remember that Jesus is the God-Man. He is as much man as he is God, yet without sin. Knowing for the first time in eternity, he will be cut off for a while from his Heavenly Father as "He has made him, who knew no sin, to be sin for us, that we might be made the righteousness of God in him" (2 Corinthians 5:21). We catch a glimpse of his agony in Matthew 26:38. "Then saith he unto them, my soul is exceedingly sorrowful, even unto death; tarry here, and watch with me." All of the disciples were with the Lord, but as he went farther into the garden, he took Peter, James, and John—three that he was especially close to in his ministry. Humanly speaking, it was a time when Jesus desperately needed and wanted prayer support. Unfortunately, the disciples, being physically tired, all fell asleep. In their defense, Jesus said, "The spirit indeed is willing, but the flesh is weak."

As I think about this request of our Lord to his disciples to watch and pray, I cannot but wonder about each of us. In my view, America as a nation is in the eleventh hour. The clock is ticking, the countdown is on. Continuing on our present course, it appears to me we are heading for destruction and the inevitable judgment of God, unless by God's grace we repent of our sin. Not since the Vietnam era has America been such a divided country. It was Jesus who said, "Every kingdom divided against itself is brought to desolation; every city or house divided against itself shall not stand" (Matthew 12:25).

The sad thing to me about where we are as a Christian nation is that, like the disciples, the Church of the Lord Jesus Christ is sound asleep. It would be wonderful to think we are just physically exhausted from serving the Lord and others, but we all know that just is not true! Unlike the disciples, we are not really willing to watch and pray. We are too wrapped up in our own little world with the center of attention on me!

The Lord is asking us today to watch and pray. Watch—for our children and grandchildren. Watch for one another and for the well-being of our nation. As we are watching and praying, be alert to the signs of the times. It is highly possible and, I believe, even likely our Lord Jesus will come soon. The admonition to every believer is to watch. "Watch therefore; for you know not what hour your Lord does come... therefore be you also ready; for in such an hour as you think not the Son of Man cometh" (Matthew 24:42–44).

Holy Ground

Second Corinthians 5:21 "For he has made him,
who knew no sin, to be sin for us, that we might
be made the righteousness of God in him."

Go with me today, in your mind's eye, to Pilate's judgment hall. "When they had twisted a crown of thorns, they put it on His head, and a reed in His right hand. And they bowed the knee before Him and mocked Him saying, 'Hail, King of the Jews!' Then they spat on Him and took the reed and struck Him on the head. And when they had mocked Him, they took the robe off Him, put His own clothes on Him, and led Him away to be crucified" (Matthew 27:29–31). "He was led as a lamb to the slaughter" (Isaiah 53:7b). "And He bearing His cross, went out to a place called the Place of a Skull, which is called in Hebrew, Golgotha, where they crucified Him, and two others with Him" (John 19:17–18). "Then two robbers were crucified with Him, one on the right hand and another on the left" (Matthew 27:38). He was numbered with the transgressors" (Isaiah 53:12).

See Jesus on Calvary's cross, dying in our place. The scripture gives us some insight to his agony and suffering. "I am a worm, and no man; a reproach of men and despised by the people. All those who see me ridicule me; they shoot out the lip, they shake the head saying, 'He trusted in the Lord, let Him rescue Him. Let Him deliver Him, since He delights in Him.' But you are He who took me out of the womb. You made me trust while on my mother's breast. I was cast upon you from birth, from my mother's womb. You have been my God, be not far from me. They gape at me with their mouths like a raging and roaring lion. I am poured out like water, and all my bones are out of joint; my heart is like wax; it has melted within me. My strength is dried up like a potsherd, and my tongue clings to my jaws; you have brought me to the dust of death. For dogs have surrounded me; the congregation of the wicked has enclosed me. They pierced my hands and my feet. I can count all my bones. They look and stare at me. They divide my garments among them, and for my clothing they cast lots." This passage taken from Psalm 22, depicting our Lord's suffering on Calvary's cross, atoning for our filthy sins, was foretold hundreds of years before it happened.

Hear the prayer of his heart in this difficult hour when he cried to the Heavenly Father, "My God, my God, why have You forsaken me?" His human suffering as the God-Man was beyond our comprehension, but to be forsaken by his Father even for a brief time was almost more than he could possibly endure. Being ordained as the Lamb slain before the foundation of the world, the Lord Jesus knew our Heavenly Father would have to allow him to experience the full fury of God's wrath in paying for our sin on the cross. God had to treat him as you and I should be treated without God's amazing grace. Someone well said that God had to forsake Jesus, so he would never have to forsake a sinner who would repent of his or her sin and place his or her faith and trust in the finished work of Christ. The Bible says, "He is also able to save to the uttermost those who come to God through Him, since He always lives to make intercession for them" (Hebrews 7:25).

On the cross, our long-suffering Savior satisfied God's law's demand and completed the work for our redemption. "He shall see the labor of His soul and be satisfied. By His knowledge, my righteous servant shall justify many for He shall bear their iniquities" (Isaiah 53:11). Therefore, Jesus could cry from the cross, "It is finished." Our sin debt was paid in full. Hallelujah!

Blessed Redeemer

Psalm 69:20 "Reproach has broken my heart and I am full
of heaviness; and I looked for some to take pity, but there
was none; and for comforters, but I found none."

In my mind, these words are indisputably the words of our Lord
voiced to our Heavenly Father from the depths of his great heart
and soul. Psalm 69:21 "They gave me also gall for my food and in
my thirst they gave me vinegar to drink." This verse confirms that
this prayer took place as our Lord hung on the cruel cross of Calvary
where he was crucified; dying so we may live, paying for our sin with
his own blood so that we would not have to pay for our sin debt. (I
owed a debt I could not pay; he paid a debt he did not owe.)

We should ever be mindful that Jesus was as much God as he
was man and as much man as he was God, yet without sin. When
we consider the agony, pain, heartache, sorrow, and loneliness he
endured in order to redeem us from sin and the curse of the law, we
should bow our heart in humility, praise, and thanksgiving for such
a blessed Savior as our Lord Jesus Christ. Isaiah reminds us, "He is
despised and rejected of men, a man of sorrows and acquainted with
grief" (Isaiah 53:3a). In the Gospel of John, the Bible tells us that our
wonderful Savior "came unto His own and His own received Him
not" (John 1:11).

When we consider how utterly sinful we are, it is difficult to
truly understand the love of God for us found only in and through
the Lord Jesus Christ. He made his soul an offering for our sin, fulfilling all the demands of God's law such as "The soul that sins must
die" or "I will in no wise clear the guilty." Scripture confirms the

sacrifice Jesus made on the cross more than satisfied the burden of the law.

"He shall see of the travail of His soul, and shall be satisfied; by His knowledge shall my righteous servant justify many; for He shall bear their iniquities" (Isaiah 53:11). In addition, we recall his last words from the cross, "It is finished" (John 19:30). Thank God, though his own people, the Jews, rejected him, just as millions from all nations reject him today, still, we who are believers can claim the promise, "As many as received Him, to them gave He the power to become the children of God. Even to them that believe on His Name; who were born, not of blood, nor of the will of the flesh, nor of the will of man, but of God" (John 1:12–13).

"Thanks be to God for His unspeakable gift" (2 Corinthians 9:15).

Resurrection

John 11:25–26 "I am the resurrection and the life. He who believes in Me, though he may die, he shall live. And whoever lives and believes in Me shall never die. Do you believe this?"

What an astounding promise this is to every believer! The promise is from very God incarnate, our blessed Lord Jesus Christ. "I am the resurrection!" You recall when God called Moses to lead his children, Israel, out of Egypt, Moses asked God how he should reply when they asked his name. "And God said to Moses, 'I am who I am.' And He said, 'Thus you shall say to the children of Israel, "I Am has sent me to you."'" Here in our text verse, Jesus says to Martha and to us, "I Am the resurrection and the life."

The same great "I Am", the Alpha and Omega, the first and the last, the beginning and the end, is the giver of eternal life through Jesus Christ and our eternal assurance of resurrection life. We know "it is appointed for man to die once" (Hebrews 9:27). However, we have the promise, though we may die, we shall live because he lives. Death could not hold its prey, Jesus. And death will not be able to hold the believer.

In the story of Lazarus, Jesus does not ask Martha to wait for the future resurrection of the dead, neither does he ask this of us, for the promise is "whoever lives and believes in Me shall never die." We may pass briefly through the valley of the shadow of death, but we will walk hand in hand with our blessed Lord into the brightness of eternity. The mortal (physical) body may die for a while, but our eternal soul will never die!

Bless God, if death comes our way, should the Lord delay his return, even this old sinful body of corruption will be changed into a glorious body like Jesus. "Behold, I tell you a mystery: we shall not all sleep, but we shall all be changed … in a moment, in the twinkling of an eye, at the last trumpet. For the trumpet will sound, and the dead will be raised incorruptible, and we shall be changed. For this corruptible must put on incorruption, and this mortal must put on immortality, then shall be brought to pass the saying that is written 'Death is swallowed up in victory. O death, where is your sting? O grave, where is your victory.' The sting of death is sin, and the strength of sin is the law. But thanks be to God who gives us the victory, through our Lord Jesus Christ" (1 Corinthians 15:51–57).

"Now Christ is risen from the dead, and has become the first fruits of those who have fallen asleep. For as in Adam all die, even so in Christ all shall be made alive" (1 Corinthians 15:20–22). "Therefore my beloved brethren, be steadfast, immovable, always abounding in the work of the Lord, knowing that your labor is not in vain in the Lord" (1 Corinthians 15:58).

Salvation, Sure and Certain

Our scriptures for the next few weeks are taken from 1 John 3:18 through 24.

> First John 3:23–24 "This is His commandment, that we should believe on the name of His Son, Jesus Christ, and love one another, as He gave us commandment. And He that keeps His commandments dwells in Him, and He in Him. And by this we know that He abides in us, by the Spirit whom He has given us."

John is the disciple who stresses the importance of love and assurance. Love first to God, and then to one another. It is probable that when John wrote this Epistle, he was addressing some who had a wavering faith. In the early days of the Church, we know there was a lot of heresy, just as there is today. In addition, society was very divided as to who Jesus really was, so at least part of John's purpose in this Epistle was to emphasize the truth about our Lord and to offer assurance to those having doubts. He seems to summarize this clearly in 1 John 5:13, "These things I have written to you who believe in the name of the Son of God, that you may know that you have eternal life, and that you may continue to believe in the name of the Son of God."

One of the key words in this passage we know is the word *believe*. Millions today believe in Jesus intellectually; that is, to acknowledge him as the Son of God, yet never committing their hearts and lives to him. The Bible tells us that even the demons believe in God. "You believe there is one God; you do well. The demons also believe and tremble" (James 2:19). Salvation comes to those who recognize their sinfulness and the need for forgiveness and a transformed life. This can only come to those who are willing to turn from sin to the Savior, believing that on Calvary's cross, he took upon himself all of our sin, paying our sin debt in full with his own precious blood. Jesus is the one and only way for any of us to gain entry into heaven and receive eternal life, which he imparts by grace to all who will come to him. "As many as received Him, to them He gave the right to become children of God, to those who believe in His name, who were born, not of blood, nor of the will of the flesh, nor of the will of man, but of God" (John 1:12).

The door to our heart is locked from within; we must open the door in order to receive him into our hearts and lives. "Behold, I stand at the door and knock; if any man hears my voice, and opens the door, I will come in to Him, and will sup with Him and he with me" (Revelation 3:20). Should anyone be reading these words today who have never invited Christ in their heart, if the Lord is speaking to you today, I urge you to open the door of your heart and receive him as your Savior. More importantly, the Lord is personally inviting you in his Word to come to him. "The Spirit and the bride say, come. And let him that hears say, come. And let him that is athirst come. And whosoever will, let him take the water of life freely" (Revelation 22:17).

Waiting on God

Lamentations 3:25 "The Lord is good unto those who wait for him, to the soul that seeks him."

In this fast-paced society in which we live, it is a challenge for each of us to be patient, to wait. We may be in line at a fast-food chain restaurant, at the post office, or some retail store, and if the attendant does not get to us quickly enough, we become impatient, sometimes even angry and wonder why they don't have more help. At a restaurant, we expect the waiter or waitress to come to our table in two minutes or less. And don't allow some slowpoke to get in front of us while driving and in our usually "hurry"—to go where? The next time some elderly person in front of you is driving slowly, may you remember if it is a gentleman, he may be a veteran who put his life on the line for you and for me. If it is a lady, it may be someone's dear mother or grandmother simply trying to keep her independence, a direction in which we are all heading rapidly.

In the spiritual realm, we struggle with the same impatience. When we bring a petition to the Lord, we expect him to act promptly; after all, we are busy people. Sometimes, like Abraham and Sarah, our lack of patience in waiting on God causes us to take matters into our own hands, resulting in one big mess. It takes discipline and time to wait on the Lord, but the rewards of waiting are many.

The psalmist encourages us, "Wait on the Lord; be of good courage and He shall strengthen thine heart, wait, I say, on the Lord" (Psalm 27:14). I wonder how many blessings of God we miss out on by failing to spend quiet time alone with him every day, seeking his presence and will for the task at hand, allowing him to speak to our hearts through his Spirit and his Word.

This matter of waiting on God has been a difficulty for God's children for many years. Many Old Testament saints struggled with this issue. Listen to a psalm, probably written by King David, "Hide not thy face from me in the day when I am in trouble; incline thine ear unto me; in the day when I call, answer me speedily," (Psalm 102:2). Aren't we just like that? We get in trouble, usually from our own misdeeds, then we pray and want God to bail us out quickly. Part of our problem often is our failure to be walking with the Lord as we should. "Wait on the Lord and keep His way and He shall exalt thee to inherit the land" (Psalm 37:34). Please note the key phrase, "keep His way."

Is there a matter of importance upon which you really need an answer? Wait on the Lord! He is Lord of heaven and earth who only does great things, "able to do exceedingly abundantly above all we ask or think, according to the power that worketh in us."

"They that wait upon the Lord shall renew their strength; they shall mount up on wings like eagles; they shall run and not be weary; and they shall walk and not faint" (Isaiah 40:31).

Pride, the Enemy of Revival

Proverbs 16:18 "Pride goeth before destruction
and an haughty spirit before a fall."

Anyone serious about living a consecrated life for the Lord must deal with pride. It is one of the major causes of the downfall of many Christians. How many godly men, even some serving God faithfully, have been taken in by the subtle flattery of a woman other than their wives, resulting in unfaithfulness to God, their wife and family. We all have witnessed those called to God's work, who lost their ministry and their testimony. What a tragedy, and all because of foolish pride. The Bible says, "A man's pride shall bring him low" (Proverbs 29:23a).

The Bible has much to say about pride, indicating to me that it is an issue we all must deal with and safeguard against. God hates pride because he knows it will keep us from yielding our stubborn will to him and ultimately cause us to self-destruct. "The fear of the Lord is to hate evil; pride and arrogance and the evil way and the perverse mouth, do I hate" (Proverbs 8:13). Personal pride can keep us from doing what God moves in us to do.

It was hellish pride and jealousy that caused Cain to slay his brother, Abel. Pride and arrogance caused Pharaoh to harden his heart toward God and his servant Moses. Was it not pride that caused King David, a man after God's own heart, to take Bathsheba, the wife of his faithful servant Uriah? "Before destruction, the heart of man is haughty" (Proverbs 18:12a). God says, "An high look and proud heart and the plowing of the wicked are sin" (Proverbs 21:4).

The consequences of pride are devastating. Cain was driven from the presence of God to be a fugitive and wanderer on the earth. In his own words, "My punishment is greater than I can bear" (Genesis 4:13). Because of pride, Pharaoh lost his son, his army, and his life. David, after committing adultery and murder, saw judgment come to his own household, lost the joy of his salvation, and, I believe, was never the same.

May God help us one and all to swallow false pride, confess our sin, and return to him. "He that covereth his sins shall not prosper, but whoever confesses and forsakes them shall have mercy" (Proverbs 28:13). If every child of God would respond favorably to the prompting of the Holy Spirit, whether it is an altar call or otherwise, revival would break out in our midst.

A Call to Repentance and Prayer

Psalm 79:9 "Help us, O God of our salvation, for the glory of thy name; and deliver us and purge away our sins, for thy name's sake."

If ever there was a time for the people of God, in this generation, to awake from slumber, to repent of sin, to return to Almighty God in humility and earnest prayer for deliverance, it is *now!* Apathy among Christians is widespread as we watch the moral decay of our society become more evident every day. The foundation of our spiritual heritage is crumbling before our very eyes while the "Church" goes on in its pleasures and sin. Like Israel of old during the Exodus, we have become idolaters!

"Neither be you idolaters, as were some of them; as it is written, the people sat down to eat and drink, and rose up to play" (1 Corinthians 10:7). The children of Israel made a golden calf and worshipped it during the Exodus from Egypt. Christians in America have idols—material things; worldly pleasures, sports, celebrities, and sex.

Do we not really care that the foundation of this country is being destroyed? The scripture reminds us, "If the foundations be destroyed, what can the righteous do?" (Psalm 11:3). If America continues on its present course, it will be without hope because it is has become a nation without God. We can complain and say our problems are political, with liberals being blamed, and yes, Satan is using everything and everyone at his disposal, including politicians, corrupt judges, the media, etc., to bring ruin to this land we love. The reality, however, is that "we" are the problem. Hear God's Word. "Help, Lord, for the godly man ceaseth; for the faithful fail from among the children of men" (Psalm 12:1). Most men will proclaim every one his own goodness; but a faithful man, who can find?" (Proverbs 20:6).

The one and only hope for us individually and as a nation is Almighty God. We need an outpouring of his precious Holy Spirit to convict us and purge our sins away, bringing about a national revival among God's people. Let the cry of our heart be to God, "Revive us and we will call upon thy name" (Psalm 80:18b). "Will thou not revive us again, that thy people may rejoice in thee?" (Psalm 85:6). "Restore us, O God and cause thy face to shine and we shall be saved" (Psalm 80:3).

Throughout our existence as a nation, we have been abundantly blessed by God, primarily because he has been our God. "Blessed is the nation whose God is the Lord; and the people whom he has chosen for his own inheritance" (Psalm 33:12). God does not owe America anything. In fact, Billy Graham said, "If God doesn't judge America, he will have to apologize to Sodom and Gomorrah." The only thing I believe that will stay the hand of God and not cause him to abandon us as a nation is if we individually and corporately repent of our sin and cry out to him in prayer to spare our land. The issue at hand is urgent, time is short. Pray that God will move throughout the body of believers in our land to bring about revival for "His Name's Sake."

The Brevity of Life

Psalm 90:10 "The days of our life are threescore years and ten; and if by reason of strength they be fourscore years, yet is their strength, labor and sorrow; for it is soon cut off, and we fly away."

In our youth, few of us ever gave thought as to how short life really is. Busy with raising our families and working hard to provide for their needs, life just seemed as though it would go on forever. Those we knew, whether family or friends who reached the milestone of threescore and ten (seventy years old) may not be around long, but not so for us—or so we thought! Now as I write these words, many of us, by the grace of God, have reached that milestone. It is nothing short of amazing when we realize how quickly the years have gone by. James said it well when he asked the question, "For what is your life? It is even a vapor that appeareth for a little time and then vanishes away" (James 4:14b).

What splendid advice the Lord gives us in this regard. The psalmist offers up a prayer from his heart, "So teach us to number our days, that we may apply our hearts unto wisdom" (Psalm 90:12). What does it mean to number our days? We have no idea just how much time God will give us on this earth, and that is really a good thing. Our time is in his hands, as well it should be. To me, the idea is to make every day count for the Lord. "Whatsoever they hand findeth to do, do it with thy might" (Ecclesiastes 9:10). It is crucial that our priorities be in proper order: God first, family, others, and self—last.

Putting God first is more than simply attending church on a regular basis, although if he is first in our lives, we will not forsake the assembling of ourselves together with fellow believers, but it is also spending quality time daily with him as well. In doing this, we will get to know him and find that he alone is the "friend that sticks closer than a brother." The best way to accomplish this is through daily Bible study and prayer.

In Revelation, chapter 2, the Lord addressed the church at Ephesus, which had an abundance of good qualities, but their failure was they had left their first love—Jesus. Neglecting to spend time with the Lord regularly will inevitably result in our failure also. Jesus warned us this would happen in the last days when he said, "Because iniquity shall abound, the love of many shall grow cold" (Matthew 24:12). Is this not the single major problem among the people of God today? We have embraced the sins of the world, the lust of the flesh, the lust of the eyes, and the pride of life. In many cases, believers are living the same way nonbelievers live, and no one can see any difference between them. Consequently, we have lost our influence on society and a lost and dying world. The Word of God has the answer. "Come out from among them and be ye separate, saith the Lord and touch not the unclean thing: and I will receive you," (2 Corinthians 6:17).

Act Now

Isaiah 55:6–7 "Seek ye the Lord while he may be found, call ye upon him while he is near; Let the wicked forsake his way, and the unrighteous man his thoughts, and let him return unto the Lord, and he will have mercy upon him; and to our God; for he will abundantly pardon."

In my view, time is running out for all of mankind. In light of the conditions in our world, everything seems to point to the imminent return of the Lord. America is on a fast track to self-destruction, which began in the sixties and continues to escalate every year. The stench of our sin must make God sick and surely reminds him of Sodom and Gomorrah. We are a sinful society where perversion, violence, greed, corruption, lust, immorality, and filthiness are prevalent.

One can but wonder for just how long the Lord will give a word of encouragement for mankind to seek him. It will not be forever, for the Bible says, "My Spirit shall not always strive with man" (Genesis 6:3a). The problem today is that few, if any, are seeking God. "The Lord looked down from Heaven upon the children of men, to see if there were any that did understand, and seek God. They are all gone aside, they are all together become filthy; there is none that doeth good, no, not one" (Psalm 14:2–3).

Sadly enough, in today's society, few professing Christians spend any time seeking God. Like Esau, we have sold our birthright for the things of the world and the pleasures of sin for a season. While our children and grandchildren are being seduced by the world, the flesh and the devil, many professing Christians (parents and grandparents alike) are asleep, wrapped up in themselves and their worldly pleasures.

Please know that I fully realize God has a remnant of faithful servants, like those in Sardis, who "have not defiled their garments" (Revelation 3:4). Thank God if you are among that number, for you are salt and light in the midst of a dark and perishing world.

Even in the midst of all the wickedness God extends, for now, his mercy and grace to saint or sinner alike. If you know him as Savior, but you are not walking close to him, he urges you today to return to him where you can find mercy and pardon afresh and anew. On the other hand, to refuse his invitation could be disastrous. "Because I have called and you refused... I have stretched out my hand and no man regarded... you would have none of my reproof... I will mock when your fear cometh... then shall they call on me, but I will not answer; they shall seek me early but they shall not find me... because they hated knowledge and did not choose the fear of the Lord" (Proverbs 1:24–29).

"Wherefore, as the Holy Spirit saith, today if you will hear His voice, harden not your heart" (Hebrews 3:7 and 8a). "For He saith, I have heard thee in a time accepted and in the day of salvation have I helped thee; behold now is the accepted time; behold now is the day of salvation" (2 Corinthians 6:2).

Offer Praise

Psalm 113:2–3 "Blessed be the Name of the Lord from this time forth and for evermore. From the rising of the sun unto the going down of the same, the Lord's Name is to be praised."

One of the weak links in our lives is our failure to offer praise and thanksgiving daily to our Lord and Savior, Jesus Christ. How many of us took time this morning just to praise him for who he is? We get so wrapped up in our own needs and concerns we neglect praise and worship. Yet it is one of the few things we can do that brings glory to his name. "Whoever offers praise glorifieth me; and to him that ordereth his conduct aright will I show the salvation of God." (Psalm 50:23).

Regardless as to where we are today and what our circumstances may be, we have much to praise God for. First and foremost in my mind is for the gift of his Son, the Lord Jesus Christ. I am reminded of the words of the angel hundreds of years ago, "Thou shall call His Name Jesus; for He shall save His people from their sins" (Matthew 1:21b). Our Heavenly Father certainly did not have to send his only Son to redeem us from sin, but he did. "Herein is love, not that we loved God, but that He loved us, and sent His Son to be the propitiation for our sins" (1 John 4:10).

When we consider how lost we were, the sinfulness of our wicked hearts, the eternal destiny of our souls before Christ saved us, we should all bow in humble adoration to offer praise to God for his "unspeakable gift." Amazing grace, how sweet the sound that saved a wretch like me, I once was lost, but now I am found, was blind, but now I see.

One of my favorite psalms is Psalm 103 because it captures so many truths of our great salvation provided by God, the Father through the Lord Jesus Christ. Here are a few. "He forgives all our iniquities, heals all our diseases, redeemed our lives from destruction, crowns us with loving-kindness and tender mercies, satisfies us with good things, He is slow to anger and plenteous in mercy, has not dealt with us after our sins nor rewarded us according to our iniquities, as the heavens are high above the earth, so great is His mercy toward them that fear Him. As far as the East is from the West, so far has he removed our transgressions from us. The mercy of the Lord is from everlasting to everlasting upon those who fear Him, and His righteousness unto children's children."

No wonder then that the Psalm begins appropriately with these words, "Bless the Lord, O my soul, and all that is within me, bless His Holy Name. Bless the Lord, O my soul and forget not all His benefits" (Psalm 103:1–2).

May we join our hearts today in praise to him for he is worthy!

God, Our Hope

Psalm 42:5 'Why art thou cast down. O my soul? And why are thou disquieted in me? Hope thou in God; for I shall yet praise him for the help of his countenance."

How is it with your soul this morning? Like the psalmist, are you cast down? Three different times, in verses 5 and 11 of chapter 42, and then in verse 5 of chapter 43, he asks the same question of himself. Why? All of us, at times, have experienced the anguish of being cast down, discouraged. Sometimes the storms of life come crashing in on us, and we feel alone and overwhelmed by it all. Consider some possibilities as to why we get into this frame of mind and what we can do to resolve it.

One of the first reactions, when things become distressing, is to have a pity party. Poor me, why is this happening to me? The psalmist experienced this for he says, "My tears have been my food day and night, while they continually say unto me, where is thy God?" (Psalm 42:3). Then in verse 9, "I will say unto God, my rock, why have you forgotten me? Why go I mourning because of the oppression of the enemy?" We would do well to remember God does not respond to self-pity. He responds to *faith!*

The problem the psalmist had is common to all of us when we become discouraged. We focus on self and circumstances rather than on the Lord. Instead of asking, *Why is this happening to me*, we perhaps should be asking the Lord, *What are you trying to teach me and what am I to do?* A key is that the psalmist knew better than to wallow in self-pity, and so do we. We see in our text he clearly knows to "Hope thou in God." In verse 9, he refers to God as "my rock."

It is also very significant that the outcome of all this is, "I shall yet praise him for the help of his countenance." He knows God will come through and so should we.

Some remedial suggestions: First and foremost, come clean with God. "He that covereth his sins shall not prosper, but whose confesseth and forsaketh them shall have mercy" (Proverbs 28:13). It is only when our hearts are right with God are we able to pray and seek his will. Then abandon all to him. We should not try to work things out for ourselves; we will surely fail. Rather, "Trust in the Lord with all your heart and lean not unto thine own understanding. In all thy ways acknowledge him and he shall direct thy paths" (Proverbs 3:5–6).

Lastly, focus on the Lord and appropriate by faith his promises. "Thou will keep him in perfect peace, whose mind is stayed on thee, because he trusteth in thee" (Isaiah 26:3). Some personal promises, "I will help thee" (Isaiah 41:14). "When thou passest through the waters, I will be with thee; and through the rivers, they shall not overflow thee; when thou walkest through fire, thou shalt not be burned, neither shall the flame kindle upon thee. For I am the Lord thy God, The Holy One of Israel, thy Savior" (Isaiah 43:2–3). "I will never leave thee, nor forsake thee" (Hebrews 13:5). Hope in the Lord.

Need Wisdom?

James 1:5 "If any of you lack wisdom, let him
ask of God, who giveth to all men liberally and
upbraideth not and it shall be given him."

Who among us does not need all of the wisdom we can acquire?
In this pilgrimage of life, none of us have the answers to all of
the complex circumstances we encounter. In reference to wisdom, I
am obviously not referring to secular education, though that is certainly important, but rather wisdom that enables us to live life to
its fullest for the glory of God and the wellbeing of those we love;
including ourselves. Recognizing that most of us have insufficient
wisdom, the Lord gave us the great promise in our text verse. Simply
put, if we lack wisdom, ask God for it, and he promises to give it
liberally!

To fully grasp the possibilities of this promise, please read
Proverbs, chapter 8. Here, our Lord Jesus is clearly defined as wisdom personified. Hear God's Word, "My mouth shall speak truth
and wickedness is an abomination to my lips ... counsel is mine and
sound wisdom. I am understanding; I have strength ... the Lord pos-
sessed me in the beginning of His way, before His works of old ... I
was set up from everlasting, from the beginning, or ever the earth
was." Then a promise similar to that in James is found in Proverbs
8:17, "I love those who love me and those who seek me early shall
find me."

It is important for us to discern the differences in wisdom and
especially its source. For example, there is a worldly, sensual, demonic
wisdom that comes from the enemy of our soul. "If you have bitter

envying and strife in your hearts, glory not and lie not against the truth. This wisdom descendeth not from above, but is earthly, sensual, demoniacal. For where envying and strife are, there is confusion and every evil work" (James 3:14–16).

On the other hand, wisdom from God is greatly to be desired. "The wisdom that is from above is first pure, then peaceable, gentle and easy to be entreated, full of mercy and good fruits, without partiality and without hypocrisy. And the fruit of righteousness is sown in peace by them that make peace" (James 3:17–18) Who among us would not want that kind of wisdom?

On the practical side, please allow me to suggest that in any and all matters, whether family relationships, business decisions or personal issues, before making a move, ask God for wisdom. Do not make a single decision without knowing for certain he is leading. The Lord cares more than we can even think or imagine, and he loves for us to seek his guidance. Just be sure we come to him in faith, believing He not only will hear but will lovingly respond. "Ask in faith, nothing wavering. For he that wavereth is like a wave of the sea driven in the wind and tossed. Let not that man think that he shall receive anything of the Lord" (James 1:6–7).

Work It Out

Philippians 2:12b–13 "Work out your own salvation
with fear and trembling. For it is God who works in
you both to will and to do of his good pleasure."

This is a powerful passage emphasizing the serious attitude that
each of us should have concerning God's gift of salvation. We
would do well to remember the words of Jesus who said, "You have
not chosen me but I have chosen you and ordained you, that you
should go and bring forth fruit and that your fruit should remain"
(John 15:16). God saved us to accomplish in us and through us his
good pleasure. We have made it a rather trite expression, but the
reality is that God does indeed have a plan and a purpose for each of
us. To me, that is very exciting and for as much time as I have left to
serve him, I do not want to miss a single opportunity he brings my
way.

In the weeks ahead, I pray we can explore in great detail all
that is involved for each of us in working out our salvation. As a
foundation, may I say that the scripture is not saying work for salvation. We know that is impossible for we have many references to
disprove such heresy. "For by grace are you saved through faith; and
that not of yourselves, it is the gift of God, not of works lest any
man should boast" (Ephesians 2:8–9). "Knowing that a man is not
justified by the works of the law, but by the faith of Jesus Christ, even
we have believed in Jesus Christ, that we might be justified by the
faith of Christ and not by the works of the law; for by the works of
the law shall no flesh be justified" (Galatians 2:16). Then the Holy
Spirit records for us in Romans 4:5, "To him that worketh not, but

believes on him that justifies the ungodly, his faith is counted for righteousness."

We can readily discern that our text is therefore telling us to work out the salvation that God has put into us through the new birth. We have been blessed with the abiding presence of God's Holy Spirit who indwells every believer and will lead us and help us to accomplish this. Note the scripture (Philippians 2:13) says, "It is God [God, the Holy Spirit] who works in you." He works in us first to will (desiring) and to do (obedience) the good pleasure (will) of God.

Our first checkpoint is to know the Spirit of God lives in our heart. "If any man have not the spirit of Christ, he is none of his" (Romans 8:9b). Then Apostle John gives us an encouraging word, "By this we know that he abideth in us, by the Spirit whom he has given us" (1 John 3:24b). If we are not conscious of the presence of God's Holy Spirit in our hearts, either we have never been born from above, or sin in our lives has both grieved and quenched the Holy Spirit from working in us.

Reproof

---◆---

Ephesians 5:13 "All things that are reproved are made manifest by the light; for whatever does make manifest is light."

How thankful each of us should be for reproof. It may come from a spouse, a relative, or a friend, but when given and received in the right spirit, it can be quite advantageous to our growth as a Christian. When I look back to my youth, how I would have loved for a brother in the Lord to teach me and counsel me in the things of the faith, for I knew there were many errors in my understanding of God's Word that needed reproof (correction).

Fortunately for all of us, the Lord gave us his Holy Spirit, whom the Bible says, "When He, the Spirit of truth, is come, He will guide you into all truth; for He shall not speak of Himself, but whatever He shall hear, that shall He speak; and He will show you things to come" (John 16:13). In addition to being our Supreme Teacher, the Holy Spirit does not allow God's children to stray too far without correcting them. Hebrews 12:6 "For whom the Lord loveth He chasteneth and scourgeth every son whom He receiveth." It may not always be pleasant to endure the chastening of the Lord, but it is a great assurance that we are his, and his correction is most profitable for our total well-being.

The Bible has much to say about reproof, probably because the Lord knows how quickly (and easily) we can go astray. As we study God's Holy Word, the light of truth shines upon us as our text in Ephesians indicates. The Word of God penetrates our total being (Hebrews 4:12). The question is, how will we respond to the Lord when we experience reprimand.

The appropriate attitude to have is to welcome the Lord's correction and leading. Proverbs 6:23 "For the commandment is a lamp and the law is light, and reproof of instruction are the way of life." We read in Proverbs 12:1, "Whoever loves instruction loves knowledge, but he that hates reproof is stupid." We can will to obey or not obey. However, to disregard correction is a dangerous choice. The Bible offers many words of caution concerning the foolishness of disobedience. Proverbs 15:10, "Correction is grievous unto him that forsakes the way and he that hates reproof shall die." Is this not a picture of the Church today? Many have forsaken the Lord's way for their own way. Now do not try to tell them about it because rectification to them is grievous. What is really sad is that the Lord is grieved when we are away from him!

There is a possibility, when under the continual conviction of God's Holy Spirit and one refuses to repent and obey, of crossing the invisible line between God's patience and his wrath. Proverbs 29:1, "He that being often reproved hardeneth his neck, shall suddenly be destroyed and that without remedy." This can be true for a saved man as well as a lost person, for in speaking of a backsliding Christian, John writes "There is a sin unto death, I do not say that he shall pray for it" (1 John 5:16).

Should anyone reading this be away from the Lord, may I plead with you to return to him while there is time and opportunity. Hear this fantastic invitation, "Seek ye the Lord while He may be found, call you upon Him while He is near; let the wicked forsake his way and the unrighteous man his thoughts, and let him return unto the Lord and He will have mercy upon him; and to our God for He will abundantly pardon" (Isaiah 55:6–7).

The Written Word

REPROOF

Second Timothy 4:1–2 "I charge thee, therefore, before God and the Lord Jesus Christ, who shall judge the living and the dead at His appearing and His Kingdom; preach the word; be diligent in season, out of season, reprove, rebuke, exhort with all long-suffering and doctrine."

This past week, we were privileged to have the Bailey Smith Real Evangelism conference at our church and heard outstanding preaching, including a message from Dr. Smith's young son, Josh, who preached on the effects of sin and how it can harm, not only an individual, but his family and even a whole nation. The message came from the book of Joshua, chapters 6 and 7 and tells how Achan's sin cost him his family and had tremendous impact on the entire nation of Israel.

As I listened to the message, I could but think of the impact that the sin of God's people, the Church, is having on our own nation in this twenty-first century. It is my firm personal conviction that unless we repent of our sin and return to our first love, the Lord Jesus Christ, our nation is doomed. We are self-destructing, not to mention the enemy within waiting to cause us harm.

Josh Smith cited a case in his church, MacArthur Boulevard Baptist in Irving, Texas, where he pastors and recently had to reprove a brother in the church. In our fifty years of church life, I have witnessed very few cases of a wayward child of God to be reproved although it is totally scriptural. Second Thessalonians 3:14–15 "If any man obey not our word by this epistle, note that man and have no company with him, that he may be ashamed. Yet count him not as an enemy, but admonish him as a brother." Here we have clear instruction from the Lord as to how we are to react to a disobedient brother or sister who may be bringing disgrace on the name of our Lord and his Church. We are to approach such a one firmly, but in love in an effort to reclaim him from the snare of the devil.

Another good word is found in Galatians 6:1, "Brethren, if a man be overtaken in a fault, you who are spiritual restore such an one in the spirit of meekness, considering thyself, lest though also be tempted." All of us are vulnerable to Satan's attacks of some kind. No one is exempt; especially if you are really trying to live for the Lord and trying to make a difference. Caring for one another in the Lord is vital for each of us. First John 5:16 "If any man see his brother sin a sin which is not unto death, he shall ask and he shall give him life for them that sin not unto death." The challenge to each of us is to live a life totally committed to the Lord, a life that is above reproach. This we can do only by the grace of God and the power of his Holy Spirit in our lives!

Crossing the Line

Proverbs 29:1 "He that being often reproved, hardeneth his neck, shall suddenly be destroyed and that without remedy."

This severe warning seems to be for an unsaved person or persons who, after many times being reproved by God, refuses to repent of his or her sin. Such a one crosses the line between God's patience and his wrath. We should remember that God is sovereign, and he alone knows when this occurs. In addition, we should be reminded that the Lord is "longsuffering toward us, not willing that any should perish, but that all should come to repentance" (2 Peter 3:9b). Nevertheless, individuals and nations can experience God's judgment for their sin. There are set limits as to how long the Holy Spirit may do his work of conviction in calling the lost to repentance of sin and faith in the Lord Jesus Christ. "The Lord said, My spirit shall not always strive with a man" (Genesis 6:3).

Consider Pharaoh

You remember how Almighty God dealt with Pharaoh and the Egyptian people through his servant Moses. In spite of severe plagues upon Egypt, Pharaoh continued to harden his heart, refusing to let the children of Israel go. As a result, the Bible says God "cast upon them the fierceness of His anger, wrath and indignation and trouble, by sending evil angels among them. He made a way to his anger; he spared not their soul from death, but gave their life over to the pestilence" (Psalm 78:49–50). Pharaoh along with his army was drowned in the Red Sea.

Consider Herod

Acts 12:21–23 "Upon a set day Herod, arrayed in royal apparel, sat upon his throne and made an oration unto them. And the people gave a shout, saying, it is the voice of a god and not a man. And immediately an Angel of the Lord smote him, because he gave not God the glory; and he was eaten of worms and died." Herod, like Pharaoh, crossed the line.

Consider Ephraim

Hosea the Prophet referred to the Northern Kingdom of Israel as Ephraim. In this situation, we see that even a nation of people can go too far in sin and rebellion. We find these sobering words of the Lord in Hosea 4:17–18, "Ephraim is joined to idols; let him alone. Their drink is sour; they have committed harlotry continually; her rulers love shame more than glory." In my mind, this passage could well be directed to our own country, America. Have not our people joined to idols? Are we not obsessed with material things, wealth, sports, and entertainment? Like Ephraim, the Lord is no longer worshipped and praised as he so should be. As a nation, we have left our godly Christian heritage and gone the way of the world. Never in my lifetime have I been more concerned about our future as now. How we need to pray for the will of God to be accomplished in us, individually and as a nation. The Lord may allow us to have what we deserve in a president this fall and not what we need. Pray he does not say of our nation, "America is joined to idols; let her alone."

"It is a fearful thing to fall into the hands of the living God," (Hebrews 10:31).

Sin Unto Death

First John 5:16 "If any man see his brother sin a sin
which is not unto death, he shall ask and he shall give
him life for them that sin not unto death. There is a sin
unto death; I do not say that he shall pray for it."

There is much to consider in this verse, so we will prayerfully seek
to explore some possibilities of its meaning. One thing is quite
clear; there is a sin not unto death, which, when detected in the life
of a fellow believer, we should immediately pray for such a one, asking God to forgive and restore them. This we are to do in the spirit
of humility. Galatians 6:1 "Brethren if a man be overtaken in a fault,
you who are spiritual restore such an one in the spirit of meekness,
considering thyself, lest thou also be tempted." The promise from
the Lord is that he will give life to that one. Such an action could
very well prevent a brother or sister from continuing in sin, which
could lead to an untimely death. For this reason, in 1 John 5:14, the
beloved apostle strongly encourages us to pray confidently in faith,
believing our Heavenly Father will grant the petitions we desire of
him.

All of us are subject to the constant battle between our two
natures as found in Romans 7:15–25. Knowing this, John encourages us to safeguard our walk with the Lord, keeping oneself pure and
unspotted from the world and to prayerfully watch for one another.

Then we must consider the sobering warning that there is a
sin unto death even for a believer. In this case, we are not to pray
with the same confidence for such a one. In all probability, you and
I would never know for sure when a fellow believer commits such a

sin. This is in the hands of our Sovereign God. The Bible does give us some examples to consider. In the eleventh chapter of 1 Corinthians, we learn that the Corinthian Believers, along with many of their other misdeeds, were improperly partaking of the Lord's supper. As a result, the Bible says, "For this cause many are weak and sickly and many sleep" (1 Corinthians 11:30). This to me emphasizes how severe a penalty can fall upon those who may take lightly the sacred things of God, such as Esau, who sold his birthright for a morsel of food.

In Acts 5:1–11, we find the tragic story of Ananias and Sapphira, who lied to the Holy Spirit. I encourage you to read these verses again and see how swift and severe was the judgment of God on this couple. Many in the early church were selling worldly goods and land and bringing the currency to the disciples for distribution to those in need. Ananias and Sapphira sold a piece of land and kept back some of the wealth for themselves, which was their privilege, but they indicated they gave all, thereby lying to God. As a result of their plot in lying to God, first Ananias, and a short time later, Sapphira, dropped dead! Like some in Corinth, this couple committed a sin unto death.

The surest way for any of us to avoid such a terrible plight is to stay in the center of God's will. First John 5:4 "For whatsoever is born of God overcometh the world; and this is the victory that overcometh the world, even our faith."

You Can Count

First Corinthians 12:12 "For as the body is one and
has many members and all the members of that one
body, being many, are one body, so also is Christ."

The twelfth chapter of 1 Corinthians is a marvelous word of encouragement to every believer who really desires to make a difference with his or her life. The apostle Paul draws a beautiful analogy between the human body and the Body of Christ. When understood, it is hard to imagine how many Christians would not be highly motivated to serve the Lord and use whatever gift or gifts they have for the glory of God. To that end, this "word" is prayerfully written as a means of encouragement. It is essential as we begin this study to realize it only applies to those who have trusted Christ for salvation and committed their lives to him; for we are reminded that "the natural man receiveth not the things of the Spirit of God; for they are foolishness unto him, neither can he know them because they are spiritually discerned" (1 Corinthians 2:14).

Every believer is an important member of the body of Christ. First Corinthians 12:27 "Now you are the body of Christ and members in particular." Did you ever think or perhaps hear someone say, "I cannot do anything...I am not talented." There is a difference between talents and the gifts of the Holy Spirit. Not everyone has great talent, but be assured, according to God's Word, everyone has at least one spiritual gift. Understanding what these are and using them effectively can make a difference in our lives as well as the Body of Christ but so can not using our gifts.

Our society has conditioned us mentally to believe only certain people really matter; such as the rich or wealthy, the famous, the influential or celebrities. Unfortunately, this lie has spilled over into the Church. In addition, we are inundated with advertisements that concentrate totally on the outward appearance. Americans spend millions annually attempting to avoid the inevitable aging process with the purchase of creams, pills, or plastic surgery. Vanity of vanities! The world makes the mistake of evaluating people based on the outward appearance, but thankfully, the Lord does not! The Bible says, "For the Lord seeth not as man seeth; for man looks on the outward appearance but the Lord looks on the heart" (1 Samuel 16:7b).

In laying the foundation for this study, please know God loves you just as you are and greatly desires to use you in his kingdom work. He has given us his Holy Spirit to indwell us and has gifted every believer for service to the Body of Christ. As we will see in the weeks ahead, we all may have different gifts, but that is a blessing that makes the entire body function properly as a unit when committed to him who is the Head of the Body of Christ. Do not make the mistake of wishing you had someone else's gift, for you are unique and special to God. First Corinthians 12:18 "But now God set the members every one of them in the body, as it has pleased Him." The Lord is building his church, and the gates of hell will not prevail against it.

We Are All Necessary

First Corinthians 12:18 "But now God set the members
every one of them in the body as it pleased him."

Recognizing the blessing of being a member of the body of Christ, we must go forward in faith, taking our place, appointed by God, in His body. Having received gifts from the Holy Spirit, who equips us for the work of the ministry, it is essential to define our gift or gifts and put them to work for the overall good of the body. In the twelfth chapter of 1 Corinthians, Paul clearly explains how vital every member of the human body is in order for it to function properly. The analogy he uses implies that this same thing is true for the Body of Christ. Sadly enough, there are those members who are not functioning as they should. Some are simply not walking with the Lord while others believe the church can function quite well without them. That is the devil's lie! We all need one another in the Body of Christ as emphasized in 1 Corinthians 12:21, "The eye cannot say unto the hand, I have no need of thee; nor again the head to the feet, I have no need of you." Then to further make the point, we read in 1 Corinthians 12:22, "Much more those members of the body which seem to be more feeble, are necessary."

Sometimes the word *feeble* can be a bit misleading or misunderstood. I personally like the definition, meaning "physically weak." Often our thoughts may turn to the elderly saints. Perhaps to some young and immature Christians, these may seem to be insignificant or even unnecessary in our society, but quite the opposite is true, just as in Paul's analogy of the human body. May we never forget it was those who may now seem feeble and gave their lives in service to our

Lord who laid solid foundations for us and have left us an outstanding legacy of faith. These dear ones are often neglected in society and sometimes overlooked in the church, but not in the eyes of God, who is keeping the records on all of us. To them, the Bible offers these words of commendation and encouragement. "Those members of the body which we think to be less honorable, upon those we bestow more abundant honor" (1 Corinthians 12:23).

There is yet another significantly important group of members who may qualify for the time being as feeble, and those are the precious children in our fellowship. They are the ones we pray will carry the torch of the Gospel of Christ to future generations of a lost and dying world following their own salvation. Just as their little bodies need to grow and be nourished properly, so does their spiritual life. We need to constantly lift them up in prayer that the Lord would shelter them from the evils of this present age; teaching them God's Word and how to walk in the Spirit. Only then will they be properly prepared to take their rightful place in the Body of Christ. Proverbs 22:6 "Train up a child in the way he should go and when he is old, he will not depart from it." In the eyes of the Lord, every member of the Body of Christ, from the youngest to the oldest, is necessary and important.

Take Time to Grow

First Corinthians 3:1–3 "And I, brethren, could not speak unto
you as unto spiritual, but as unto carnal, even as unto babes in
Christ. I have fed you with milk and not with solid food; for to
this time you were not able to bear it, neither yet now are you able.
For you are yet carnal; for whereas there is among you envying
and strife and divisions, are you not carnal and walk as men."

While this passage was written by Apostle Paul, inspired by
the Holy Spirit to the church at Corinth, the distress Paul
expresses is a great concern to many of us today. It has been a topic
of discussion of late in our church and Bible study. We are aware of
the frightening statistics, particularly concerning our youth. When
college is behind them, a very small percentage of our young people, who profess faith in Christ, remain active in a Bible-believing
church. Should this trend continue, just imagine what our nation
will be like in the next twenty years.

Every one of us began as a babe in Christ, for the Bible says, "If
any man be in Christ, he is a new creation; old thing are passed away;
behold, all things are become new" (2 Corinthians 5:17). It was Jesus
who said to Nicodemus, the religious but lost Pharisee, "Marvel not
that I said unto thee, you must be born again." The word *must* here is
an imperative. Now when we receive Christ as our Lord and Savior,
we are indeed a new babe in Christ. The problem is that so many
professing saints are still in spiritual infancy, even though they are
adults. Our pastor preached a powerful message this past Sunday
morning on the lack of passion in our lives for the Lord. (This mes-

sage can be heard at FBConcord.org/Worship. It will be worth your time to see it and hear it.)

Just as we all know a newborn baby needs milk, likewise, a new Christian needs to begin life with the milk of God's Word. In fact, the Bible encourages a babe in Christ. "As newborn babes, desire the pure milk of the word, that you may grow by it" (1 Peter 2:2). One of the problems facing us today, however, is that so many Christians are still drinking milk. All of the spiritual food they get is the spoon-feeding on Sunday morning if they even go to church. Like the Corinthian church, so many who profess faith in Christ are still carnal Christians, filled with the cares and attitudes of the world. God desires us to have so much more. He wants us to feast on solid food, the meat of his Holy Word.

What parent would not want to wean their precious child from milk gradually to give them solid food in order for the baby to grow physically healthy and strong! By the same token, that is what the Lord desires for each of us. The only way we can become strong in the Lord and in the power of his might is by spending time every day in the study of his Word. It will change our lives.

Amazing Grace

Hebrews 2:9–10 "We see Jesus, who was made a little lower than the angels for the suffering of death, crowned with glory and honor, that He, by the grace of God, should taste death for every man. For it became Him, for whom are all things and by whom are all things, in bringing many sons unto glory, to make the captain of their salvation perfect through suffering."

One of the difficulties experienced weekly in writing these brief devotions is attempting to condense the great truths of scripture into a few paragraphs. Such is the case in this passage. Here we find the truly amazing grace of Almighty God as revealed in the sacrificial death of his only begotten Son, the Lamb of God, who takes away the sin of the world, our Lord Jesus Christ. By choice, he was made a little lower than the angels, in that he became obedient unto death, even the death of the cross. This is truly amazing when you consider what is mentioned in this passage. All things are for him and all things are made by him.

Please note that he tasted death, not for a select few, but rather for every man (John 3:16). For the Bible says the Lord is "not willing that any should perish but that all should come to repentance" (2 Peter 3:9b). It is through our Lord's atoning death, and no other way, that you and I can be redeemed. For the Bible says, "Neither is there salvation in any other; for there is no other name under heaven given among men, whereby we must be saved" (Acts 4:12). I am reminded of a beautiful song whose chorus asks the question, "Why should He love me so, why should He love me so? Why should my Savior to

Calvary go? Why should He love me so?" My heart tells me it is for one reason only, and that is because of *his amazing grace!*

Our text tells us Jesus is crowned with glory and honor. The truth of the text is further expressed in Revelation 4:11, "Thou art worthy O Lord, to receive glory and honor and power; for thou has created all things and for thy pleasure they are and were created." Everything belongs to the Lord, including the redeemed, for we have been bought with his own precious blood. He did not have to die for us, but he did. He did not have to redeem us, but he did. Concerning his death, he said, "Therefore does my Father love me, because I lay down my life, that I might take it again. No man takes it from me, but I lay it down of myself. I have power to lay it down and I have power to take it again. This commandment have I received of my Father" (John 10:17–18). He did not have to love us, but praise God he did and he does—eternally.

We can join with the Father and Holy Spirit in proclaiming that he is worthy of all power and glory. "Wherefore, God also has highly exalted Him and given Him a name which is above every name, that at the name of Jesus every knee should bow, of things in heaven and in earth and things under the earth, and that every tongue should confess that Jesus Christ is Lord to the glory of God the Father" (Philippians 2:9–11).

He gave his all that we may become children of God, heirs of the promises, sons brought to glory—an amazing act of love and grace.

Give Thanks

Psalm 95:1–3 "Oh, come, let us sing unto the Lord;
let us make a joyful noise to the rock of our salvation.
Let us come before His presence with thanksgiving and
make a joyful noise unto Him with psalms. For the Lord
is a great God and a great King above all gods."

The giving of thanks to the Lord should be as natural to every Christian as breathing, but I fear we are often negligent in this area of our lives, just as we are in our prayer life. Ingratitude can be traced back as far as the Garden of Eden where, in a virtual paradise, man's corrupt heart chose to satisfy his own selfish desires, plunging the human race into sin! Then I am reminded when Jesus was here on earth, how ten lepers came to ask him to heal them (Luke 17:11–19). Jesus, in mercy, healed all ten, but only one, a Samaritan, returned to give glory to God. "And Jesus, answering said, 'Were not ten cleansed? But where are the nine?'" As we each search our hearts, let us ask the question, "Which group would I fit into? The nine ungrateful ones or the one who gave thanks to God?"

Sometimes life brings us difficult situations to deal with and the giving of thanks is challenging, or it may not even be on our mind. However, as difficult as it may be, our obedience to God in giving thanks will make a difference in our heart and life. First Thessalonians 5:18 reminds us, "In everything give thanks; for this is the will of God in Christ Jesus concerning you." Please note two crucial things. First, we give thanks "in everything," not "for everything." Secondly, it is God's will that we give thanks even in the midst of our trials. This will strengthen our faith.

So as we come upon this season of the year where we set aside a particular day for Thanksgiving, may we join our hearts together in the giving of thanks. "Oh, magnify the Lord with me and let us exalt his name together" (Psalm 34:3). May the Lord help us to do this daily, not just once a year. After all, the Bible says, "Blessed be the Lord, who daily loadeth us with benefits, even the God of our salvation" (Psalm 68:19).

While we sometimes want to offer thanks for material things and financial blessings at this time of year, I would like to encourage each of us to focus on and be thankful to our Heavenly Father, the Source of all blessings. James 1:17 "Every good gift and every perfect gift is from above and cometh down from the Father of lights, with whom there is no variableness, neither shadow of turning."

The most perfect gift to the world was his only Son, our Lord Jesus, who was rich, yet for our sake became poor that we, through his poverty, might be rich. "Thanks be to God for his unspeakable gift" (2 Corinthians 9:15).

Kathy and I want to wish you and your family a very blessed and happy Thanksgiving.

Great Is Thy Faithfulness

Lamentations 3:22–23 "It is because of the Lord's mercies that we are not consumed, because His compassions fail not. They are new every morning; great is thy faithfulness."

My sweet wife prepared a great meal for me on Sunday with one of my favorite desserts. We usually eat out on Sunday, but she had our daughter and our two grandchildren over to celebrate Papa's seventieth birthday, which was Wednesday of last week (October 31). It is hard to believe I am as old as I am. God has blessed me with good health and a sound mind through these many years, for which I am grateful. I am reminded of the brevity of life, however, and what James wrote when he said, "What is your life? It is even a vapor that appeareth for a little time and then vanishes away" (James 4:14b). The years have passed so quickly.

For some unknown reason, while working in the yard this past week, I began to reflect on my life. In particular, I thought on the lines of the text. Were it not for the compassion of the Lord, his wonderful mercy and grace, my life could have been a disaster like so many today. His mercy has kept each of us, who know him, from being consumed by the world, the flesh, and the devil. It is because his compassions fail not. The psalmist said it far better than I could, "As a father pities his children, so the Lord pities them that fear him. For He knoweth our frame; He remembers that we are dust" (Psalm 103:13–14).

Some of you may remember the song we sang many years ago titled "Without Him." One line near the end says, "Without Him how lost I would be." How very true that is. Not only is the Lord's mercy and compassion unfailing, but as an added blessing, they are *new* every morning. Fresh mercy, fresh compassion—at our disposal by God's grace every morning of our lives. Like daily manna sent down to us from our Heavenly Father. Oh, that we might learn to believe and claim that great truth. It can truly make a profound difference in our lives.

So many times God's children get hung up on past sin and failures. Satan, the enemy of our soul, loves for us to look back for through this method, he can steal one's joy. I remind you that our compassionate and loving Heavenly Father has provided the remedy, which is the precious blood of our Lord Jesus. "If we confess our sins, he is faithful and just to forgive us our sins and to cleanse us from all unrighteousness ... for the blood of Jesus Christ, His Son, cleanses us from all sin" (1 John 1:7b and 9). In his faithfulness, we are continually cleansed by the blood immediately upon confession of our sin. (So stop looking in the rearview mirror.)

Some of you today are anxious and worried over difficulties you are facing. May I encourage you with this verse from 1 Peter 5:7, "Casting all your cares upon Him; for He cares for you." Take him at his word today. Believe his Word; trust his grace. Do not be robbed of the joy of the Lord, but take your daily portion of his compassion and mercy, and may the *joy* of the Lord be your strength today.

A Blessed Membership

First Corinthians 12:20 "Now are they many
members, yet but one body."

It seems to me that we all have an inborn desire and even a need to
be accepted, to be loved. On occasion, perhaps like me, you may
have observed some young people often wearing black and having
dyed their hair an unnatural color. They seem to be crying out for
attention, wanting to be noticed, but certainly missing the mark.
One reason so many youngsters today join a gang is because they
want to be a part of a group where they will be accepted and feel that
they belong. Often the love and affection they seek is not found at
home.

Most of us in our youth, while in school, were members of some
organization. Perhaps it was band, choral group, or maybe a sorority
or fraternity. In our society today, there are clubs and organizations
with an elite membership. Only certain privileged ones can belong.
However, in God's amazing economy, everyone who is born again is
a "member" of the body of Christ, the Church. There is only one way
to obtain membership, and that is through saving faith in the Lord
Jesus. When we make that commitment, the Bible says we become
"accepted in the beloved" (Ephesians 1:6). I would rather belong to
the Lord Jesus and be a member of the Body of Christ than belong to
the most prestigious or exclusive group in the world, wouldn't you?

May we never take our membership in the Body of Christ for
granted, for while salvation is a free gift to us by grace through faith,
it cost the Heavenly Father his one and only son. Peter reminds us
in 1 Peter 1:18–19, "You know that you were not redeemed with

corruptible things, like silver and gold, from your vain manner of life received by tradition from your fathers, but with the precious blood of Christ, as of a lamb without blemish and without spot."

Membership in the Body carries a huge responsibility for each of us. Having been purchased by the Lord Jesus, bought back from sin and destruction, we will be held accountable for the things done in our bodies and our service to the Lord. First Corinthians 6:19–20 "What, know you not that your body is the temple of the Holy Spirit who is in you, whom you have of God and you are not your own? For you are bought with a price, therefore glorify God in your body and in your spirit, which are God's." Here in this verse is a glaring truth few Christians believe and practice. "You are not your own."

What a revival we would experience, first in our own hearts and lives and then throughout the body of Christ, if every member truly believed this great truth. While you and I cannot cause others to believe this truth, we can believe it for ourselves and practice it in our daily living. I submit to you, it is the only way we will personally experience God's peace, which passes all understanding and have unspeakable joy. May the Lord grant this victory to each of us so that we may glorify him fully as a member of his Body.

Shared Suffering

First Corinthians 12:26 "And whether one member
suffer, all the members suffer with it; or one member
be honored, all the members rejoice with it."

As it relates to the human body, I had a personal experience with
the first part of the truth in this verse; that of one member suffering and all members suffering with it. Perhaps some of you have as
well. In my senior year of high school, while living in New Orleans,
I worked in the stockroom of a five-and-dime. (This was also where
I met my sweet wife of fifty-one years. Neither of us knew the Lord
at the time.) Through a freak accident at work, I severed the tip of
my ring finger on my left hand, right below the fingernail. The store
manager drove me to the company doctor's office where the doctor
gave me a shot of Novocain, stitched and dressed my finger. Because
of the numbing effect of the Novocain, and being so early in the day,
I went back to work even though the manager recommended my
going home. However, around three o'clock in the afternoon, the
Novocain began to wear off. Not only did my finger begin to throb,
but my entire body ached. Consequently, I went home; but for some
time, there was no relief from the pain. Years later, having learned
this text, I fully realized what God's Word was saying. Here, a very
small part of one member of my body was suffering, yet my entire
body suffered with it.

The blessed Holy Spirit is saying to each of us, concerning the
fellowship of believers, that it is exactly how we are supposed to react
when our brothers or sisters in Christ are hurting. Paul puts it in simple words in Romans 12:15–16, "Rejoice with them that do rejoice

and weep with them that weep. Be of the same mind one toward another. Mind not high things but condescend to men of low estate. Be not wise in your own conceits." If you have never yet walked through the valley of suffering, pain, and sorrow, be sure that at some point you will. It is part of life! What a joy and comfort it is to our hearts; however, to know that as a child of God, we never have to go through those difficult days alone, for our Lord has promised in his Word, "I am with thee and will keep thee in all places" (Genesis 28:15). We have the great promise to each of us concerning God's Holy Spirit. John 14:16–18 "I will pray the Father and he shall give you another Comforter, that he may abide with you forever. Even the Spirit of truth whom the world cannot receive, because it seeth him not, neither knoweth him; but you know him; for he dwells with you and shall be in you." Sometimes only the Holy Spirit can minister grace and peace to a troubled heart, but are you not thankful for Christian friends who pray for you, encourage you, and try to offer comfort and hope in troubled times? This is true ministry when we can hurt when others hurt and pray earnestly for God's comfort in their time of need. Maybe prayer is all we can offer, but what abundant power there is in prayer!

Let us take time this week to seek opportunity to minister to a fellow member enduring some type of suffering, whether it be physical or otherwise. Second Corinthians 1:3 "Blessed be God, even the Father of our Lord Jesus Christ, the Father of mercies and the God of all comfort, who comforteth us in all our tribulation, that we may be able to comfort them who are in any trouble, by the comfort with which we ourselves are comforted of God."

No Division in the Body

1 Corinthians 12:24–25 "For our comely parts have no need; but God has tempered the body together, having given more abundant honor to that part which lacked. That there should be no schism in the body, but that the members should have the same care one for another."

Paul compares the human body to the spiritual body and to me that is so profound. The Holy Spirit continues to emphasize the significance of every member. Not only is everyone of infinite worth, but just as we take great care of our human body, so are we to care for one another. Take time to read Acts 2:41–47 and see the example laid down for us by the early Church. As we look back for a moment from time to time, we see the wonderful grace and mercy of God in our lives and the caring love and concern shown us by many brothers and sisters in Christ. Consequently, we are highly motivated by the Spirit of God to be available for his use; and to also reach out in love to those whose lives we hope to touch and make a difference.

You remember, the Corinthians were a divided congregation (1 Corinthians 3:1–11). For this reason, as well as for us, Paul says the body should not be divided. The King James Version uses the word *schism*, which means "division." While I grew up with the KJV, the NIV does a good job of amplifying our text. "God has combined the members of the body and has given greater honor to the parts that lacked, so that there should be no division in the body, but that its parts should have equal concern for each other." If we are honest with ourselves and with God, we just rarely do this. It seems the modern Church is very selective as to whom it will show concern. While it is human nature to identify with and care for certain members we may be close to, there are countless numbers in our body of believers who are neglected and feel very alone and unloved. I challenge each of us this week to go out of our way to say a kind word, give a warm smile or handshake to one we may not normally pay attention to. Not only will it bless their lives but ours as well.

We are to be united in heart, mind, and purpose. It is okay to disagree as long as we are not disagreeable. When the majority in a fellowship elect to do a certain thing, having expressed our thoughts in love, we need to support the decision of the Body. No division! Being a very opinionated individual, I work hard at accepting issues I may not particularly like or agree with in a fellowship. One thing I will never do, by God's grace, is to sow discord among the brethren. This is one of the seven deadly sins that God hates. Proverbs 6:16–19, "These six things does the Lord hate, yea seven are an abomination unto him. A proud look, a lying tongue, and hands that shed innocent blood, a heart that devises wicked imaginations, feet that are swift in running to mischief, a false witness that speaks lies and he that sows discord among the brethren."

The early Church was bound together by an agape love for one another, not a selective few. Acts 2:46 "And they, continuing daily with one accord in the temple and breaking bread from house to house, did eat their food with gladness and singleness of heart." The results were that united together, they were "praising God and having favor with all the people. And the Lord added to the church daily such as should be saved" (Acts 2:47).

How Is Your Vision?

Psalm 146:8a "The Lord opens the eyes of the blind."

This is one of those verses that, in my mind, can mean two different things. For example, we know assuredly that the Lord Jesus, during his earthly ministry, gave sight to some who were blind. John 9:6–7 "When He had thus spoken, He spat on the ground and made clay of the spittle and anointed the eyes of the blind man with the clay and said unto him, go wash in the pool of Siloam [which is by interpretation, "sent"]. He went his way therefore and washed and came seeing." This is a miracle indeed in that the blind man could see with his physical eyes for the first time since his birth.

I submit to you that the Lord Jesus also opens eyes that are spiritually blind. In fact, the Bible teaches that before our conversion, every one of us is spiritually blind. This blindness is brought on by the enemy of the soul, Satan himself. Second Corinthians 4:3–4 "But if our gospel be hidden it is hidden to them that are lost. In whom the God of this age has blinded the minds of them who believe not, lest the light of the glorious gospel of Christ, who is the image of God, should shine unto them." We can never be saved until the power of God's Holy Spirit touches our spiritual eyes, and they are opened, recognizing our sinful and lost condition, whereby we then turn in repentance of sin and faith in Christ. While one may have his or her physical eyes opened for the first time, and being able to see is a marvelous thing, it pales in comparison to having the spiritual eyes open and coming to that saving faith in the Lord Jesus Christ.

As an encouragement to believers and affirming spiritual blindness to those who are lost, Paul writes in Ephesians 4:17–18, "This I say, therefore, and testify in the Lord, that you henceforth walk not as other Gentiles walk, in the vanity of their mind, having the understanding darkened, being alienated from the life of God through the ignorance that is in them, because of the blindness of their heart." I am reminded of that wonderful verse of "Amazing Grace"; "I once was blind but now I see." How we need to pray for family and friends who are blinded by the god of this world, that the scales would fall from their eyes, and the light of Christ would shine upon them.

One other major concern to me is professing Christians whose lives give little or no evidence that they belong to Christ. God only knows each heart, but the Bible says, "By their fruits you shall know them." There are rare occasions when one who has truly passed from death unto life shows little spiritual growth, and before long, they are entrapped by the cares and desires of the world and are not even sure if they are saved. A sad place to be indeed, and one that the Lord does not want the believer to be in. Please read 2 Peter 1:1–10. Peter discusses Christian virtues and then says, "For if these things be in you and abound, they make you that you shall neither be barren nor unfruitful in the knowledge of the Lord Jesus Christ. But he that lacks these things is blind and cannot see afar off and has forgotten that he was purged from his old sins."

The Cost of Unbelief

Numbers 21:5 "And the people spoke against God and Moses, wherefore have you brought us up out of Egypt to die in the wilderness? For there is no bread, neither is there any water; and our soul loatheth this light bread."

God miraculously delivered Israel from the bondage of the Egyptians and intended that Israel should march right into the Promised Land. The Lord promised the Israelites, through his servant, Moses, that he would give them the land flowing with milk and honey. Twelve spies were sent to inspect this land, and ten of the twelve brought back an evil report. As a result of their unbelief, the people roamed in the wilderness for forty years.

God pronounced a harsh judgment upon them for their sin and only excused those nineteen years and younger, in addition to Joshua and Caleb, who wanted to obey God and go directly into the Promised Land. Numbers 14:35 "I, the Lord, have said I will surely do it unto all this evil congregation, who are gathered together against me; in this wilderness they shall be consumed and there they shall die." May we learn some important lessons from this biblical history. When Almighty God gives us a promise to keep, we had best act on it. The Bible says, "To him that knoweth to do good and doeth it not, to him it is sin" (James 4:17). Failing to believe God's Word, or to claim his promises by faith, results in lost blessings and opportunities to glorify our Lord and a lack of personal fulfillment.

Hebrews 3:12 "Take heed brethren lest there be in any of you an evil heart of unbelief, in departing from the living God." While we know God is love, he also is a God of judgment. We hear very little of that in pulpits across America, but it is truth nonetheless. God loves sinners, but he hates our sin. It was our sin that nailed our Savior to the cross. We would do well to learn from this example that while God is a very patient God, it is possible to cross the line between his patience and his wrath. This is exactly what Israel did after coming out of Egypt into the wilderness.

There were constant murmurings and complaining from God's people, even to the point of saying they would like to go back to Egypt and be in bondage again. Unbelievable, considering all the Lord God had done for them. Before we are too critical, consider the many times we are very much like that today. We complain and become disgruntled over small things sometimes. How often we indict ourselves! The Bible says, "It is a fearful thing to fall into the hands of the living God" (Hebrews 10:31).

According to his Word, God brought judgment on his people in that every man who brought up an evil report concerning the Promised Land was punished. Only Joshua and Caleb, faithful believers, were spared to inherit the land. Then after God pronounced judgment on everyone twenty years and older, there was great regret. Numbers 14:39 "Moses told these sayings [God's judgment] unto all the children of Israel; and the people mourned greatly." Regret and remorse are not the same as repentance. Many today are sorry for their sin but not willing to turn (repent) from sin and commit their hearts and lives to Christ. The Israelites finally said to Moses, "Lo, we are here and will go up unto the place which the Lord has promised for we have sinned" (Numbers 14:40b).

The sad truth is they crossed the line, and God would no longer hold back judgment. Moses told them, "Go not up, for the Lord is not among you," (Numbers 14:42a).

Look and Live

Numbers 21:5–6 "And the people spoke against God and against Moses, wherefore have you brought us out of Egypt to die in the wilderness? For there is no bread, neither is there any water; and our soul loatheth this light bread. And the Lord sent fiery serpents among the people and they bit the people and many of Israel died."

Having exhausted the patience of God, Israel, as a result of their continued murmuring and complaining, received multiple judgments from God. The long-range judgment was that those twenty years and older would not enter the Promised Land; and in the short term, the Lord God sent fiery serpents to bite and kill a countless number of the people. While the judgment to keep them out of the Promised Land would not be retracted, being a God of mercy, the Lord was willing to forgive those who repented of sin after Moses interceded for them. What a great lesson this is for all who are willing to turn from sin in faith to Christ and of the enormous power of intercessory prayer. "The people came to Moses and said, we have sinned; for we have spoken against the Lord and against thee; pray unto the Lord that He take away the serpents from us. And Moses prayed for the people" (Numbers 21:7). As I read this, I wondered how many of us would intercede in prayer for our critics and those who use us. Yet I am reminded of the words of Jesus, "Love your enemies, bless them that curse you, do good to them that hate you, and pray for them who despitefully use you and persecute you" (Matthew 5:44).

"And the Lord said unto Moses, make thee a fiery serpent and set it upon a pole; and it shall come to pass that everyone that is bitten, when he looks upon it, shall live" (Numbers 21:8). The serpent here is a symbol of sin judged. It was made of bronze, which speaks of divine judgment. The bronze serpent is a type of Christ "made sin for us." In John, chapter 3, Jesus is speaking with Nicodemus, a religious but lost man, about the new birth. Realizing he knew the Old Testament story, Jesus said, "As Moses lifted up the serpent in the wilderness, even so must the Son of Man be lifted up, that whosoever believeth in him should not perish, but have eternal life" (John 3:14–15).

All of us have been bitten by sin for "all have sinned and come short of the glory of God." The Bible says, "There is none righteous, no not one." And again, the Bible says, "The wages of sin is death." Like Israel, being bitten by the fiery serpent, there is only one cure for sin in our lives. That cure is the shed blood of Christ, shed to redeem all who would come to Him in repentance and faith. Just as the promise to those bitten by the serpent in the wilderness was to "look and live," so the promise is to all today. Look to Jesus and live!

How sad it is to me that people will try everything else today to find eternal life except to look to Jesus. Religion, good works, or self-sacrifice cannot ever wash away one single sin. Why will we simply not look to Jesus and be healed? Hear the heart of God if you are without Christ. "As I live, saith the Lord God, I have no pleasure in the death of the wicked, but that the wicked turn from his way and live; turn you, turn from your evil ways; for why will you die?" (Ezekiel 33:11).

Our Enemy Is Persistent

Genesis 39:11–12 "And it came to pass about this time, that Joseph went into the house to do his work; and there was none of the men of the house there within. And she caught him by his garment saying, lie with me; and he left his garment in her hand, and fled, and got out."

Having refused to have an illicit affair with Potiphar's wife once before, she continued to try and seduce the young man daily. "And it came to pass, as she spoke to Joseph day by day, that he hearkened not unto her, to lie with her, or to be with her" (Genesis 39:10). Please note the wicked tempter set up this situation so that no men were in the house. He probably tried, though unsuccessful, to convince Joseph no one would ever know, but the Bible says, "Be sure your sin will find you out," (Numbers 32:23b).

Because of his love and commitment to the Lord, Joseph's behavior was exemplary! Notice, Joseph even refused to be with Potiphar's wife. He was not going to trust the flesh for a minute knowing her ultimate intentions. She more than likely tried to convince him he could at least spend time with her even if he did not want to have an affair with her. Joseph was so wise, for the Bible says to those who want to play with sin, "Can a man take fire in his bosom and his clothes not be burned?" (Proverbs 6:27).

On another occasion, Potiphar's wife "caught him by his garment saying, 'lie with me'; and he left his garment in her hand and fled, and got out" (Genesis 39:12). Considering his circumstances, Joseph did the wisest thing he could do—he ran! Angered by Joseph's rejection, Potiphar's wife falsely accused him, resulting in his being put in prison for many years. God, however, knew his young servant was innocent and later made Joseph the prime minister of Egypt, second only to the pharaoh in authority.

There are so many great lessons for all of us in this account for men and women. We need to be especially careful how we live and walk in this wicked world. It is dangerous to play with sin of any kind. We need to guard against ever being in a possible compromising position for Satan will surely attack. Like Joseph, even a false accusation can ruin one's life and testimony. We would do well to remember we are in spiritual warfare, and the enemy has a complete arsenal to use against us. It is not limited to matters of the flesh; he may attack our faith, our commitment, and our devotion to the Lord.

Satan never lets up; just as he persisted against Joseph, he will persist against us. Even our Lord Jesus was under constant attack. Read of his temptation in Matthew, chapter 4. The parallel passage is in Luke 4:13 where the Bible says, "When the devil had ended all the testing, he departed from him for a season. Notice "for a season." That is evidence he came back. Just as our Lord and Joseph resisted the devil, so must we. James 4:7b tells us, "Resist the devil and he will flee from you." Be sure, however, he will be back time and time again.

Helps from the Word

Second Timothy 2:22 "Flee also youthful lusts, but
follow righteousness, faith, love, peace with them
that call on the Lord out of a pure heart."

What a great word of encouragement to all of us. We have
observed in our study these past several weeks from real life
examples, the tremendous cost to those who choose the way of the
world. We have also seen in the story of Joseph, the joyous outcome
of walking with the Lord. Our text today encourages each of us to
flee from evil and follow what is right. To summarize this study, I
would like to offer some scriptural, but practical, things to consider
that will help us in our walk with the Lord.

Stay focused. Since all solicitations to depart from the Lord
and be unfaithful to him begin in our heart/mind, it stands to reason
we need to be protective of our mind and heart. "Keep thy heart with
all diligence; for out of it are the issues of life" (Proverbs 4:23). Please
note the very issues of life come from or need to be addressed in our
heart. To help us stay focused, we must train our minds to be stayed
on the Lord. "Thou will keep him in perfect peace whose mind is
stayed on thee, because he trusteth in thee" (Isaiah 26:3).

Study God's Word. "Oh, how I love thy law! It is my medita-
tion all the day" (Psalm 119:97). We cannot meditate in God's Word
if we fail to study it. Psalm 119:11 "Thy Word have I hidden in mine
heart, that I might not sin against thee."

Spend time with the Lord. "Draw near to God and He will
draw near to you" (James 4:8a). God created us to worship and have
fellowship with him. He longs for us to spend time with him. Our

Lord Jesus says, "Come unto me all you that labor and are heavy laden, and I will give you rest. Take my yoke upon you and learn of me; for I am meek and lowly in heart and you shall find rest unto your souls. For my yoke is easy and my burden is light" (Matthew 11:28–30).

Keep your guard up at all times. "Be sober, be vigilant, because your adversary, the devil, like a roaring lion walketh about seeking whom he may devour" (1 Peter 5:8). Don't be Satan's next victim, but put on the whole armor of God and be prepared (Ephesians 6:11–17).

Choose your friends wisely! "Blessed is the man who walketh not in the counsel of the ungodly, nor standeth in the way of sinners, nor sitteth in the seat of the scornful. But his delight is in the law of the Lord and in his law does he meditate day and night" (Psalm 1:1–2).

Finally, **rejoice with your wife!** Proverbs 5:18–19 "Let thy fountains be blessed and rejoice with the wife of thy youth. Let her be as the loving hind and pleasant roe; let her breasts satisfy thee at all times and be thou ravished always with her love."

Just a few words to clarify the "loving hind and pleasant roe." Obviously, in biblical days, these may have been tamed and kept as a pet. The beauty of these descriptive words are as follows: A hind was the female of the common stag. Often referred to in scripture, some of its characteristics were its gentleness, feminine modesty, shyness, and timidity. The roe, on the other hand, was a species of antelope, possibly a gazelle. The roe was celebrated for its loveliness. We can see from these poetic expressions that the writer is describing the beauty of our wives. This beautiful description goes far beyond outward appearance, which is temporal and passing, to look upon her inner beauty, which is in fact the real person. The admonition is that our God has blessed us indeed with one who is far more than our helpmeet, but the love of our life!

MARVELOUS CREATION

Genesis 1:1 "In the beginning God created
the heavens and the earth."

By his mighty power, Almighty God spoke the heavens and the earth into existence. In the first twenty-five verses of Genesis, chapter 1, we find recorded seven times the words *and God said.* This took place over a period of six days. The length of those days is a debatable subject among scholars, but to me, it is not relevant. What is very relevant is that God created, made something from nothing, with the sheer power of his spoken Word.

The sixth day was a special day because God made every living creature. "And God made the beast of the earth according to its kind, cattle according to its kind, and everything that creeps on the earth according to its kind. And God saw that it was good" (Genesis 1:25). Now we learn that on the sixth day, remarkable man was formed from the very dust of the earth by the Triune God! Man was distinct from everything else God created in that he was made in the very image of God and would become a living soul when God breathed into him the breath of life. Man would have a body, soul, and spirit and would also have intellect, emotions, and a free will.

"Then God said, let Us make man in Our image, according to Our likeness; so God created man in His own image, in the image of God He created him: male and female created he them" (Genesis 1:26–27). It is significant to know that the Father, Son, and Holy Spirit all participated in the creation of man. This truth is evidenced by this illustration of phrase, "Let Us make man in Our image," the Triune God! John the Beloved writes, "There are three that bear witness in heaven; the Father, the Word, and the Holy Spirit; and these three are one" (First John 5:7).

God gave man dominion over all the earth and over all creation. He also blessed man, telling him to be fruitful, to multiply and subdue the earth. "And God saw everything that He made and indeed it was very good. So the evening and the morning were the sixth day" (Genesis 1:31). After completing all of creation in six days, "God ended His work which He made; and He rested on the seventh day from all His work which He had made. And God blessed the seventh day and sanctified it because that in it He had rested from all His work which God created and made" (Genesis 2:2–3).

In addition to the beautiful earth he created, God planted a garden eastward in Eden. A river went out of Eden to water the garden for at this time, it had never rained, but a mist came up to water the ground. The Lord also made many trees to grow out of the ground. Some were fruit trees while others were simply pleasant to the sight for man to enjoy. In this perfect paradise, we read, "And the Lord God took the man and put him into the Garden of Eden to till it and to keep it" (Genesis 2:15).

The Garden of Eden was a gardener's dream come true. Just imagine, no weeds, no thorns or any other nuisance to deal with. Keeping the garden would be easy and most enjoyable. This is evidence of God's creative perfection, his love and grace shown to man by giving him such a beautiful environment.

Our Journey to the Cross ... and Beyond

APPARENT CHAOS

Jeremiah 4:23 "I beheld the earth and indeed
it was without form and void."

The words *without form and void* express the concept of chaos. Some scholars believe the earth (not the universe) was reduced to this state after its original creation. In our closing verse from last week, let us recall these words, "For thus saith the Lord, who created the heavens, who is God, who formed the earth and made it, who did not create it in vain, who formed it to be inhabited" (Isaiah 45:18). May we be reminded that the word *create* means to make something from nothing. This is evident in Psalm 33:6 and 9. "By the word of the Lord, the heavens were made, and all the host of them by the breath of His mouth. For He spoke and it was done; He commanded and it stood fast."

Assuming scholars are correct, and God alone knows for certain, seemingly after God originally created the earth, something happened, causing it to be "without form and void." The word *was* in Genesis 1:2 is translated *became*, so sometime after God created the earth, it later *became* without form and void. Assuming this to be accurate, one must ask, what created this occurrence? This is where the divine judgment interpretation enters the picture. Events took place in heaven having great significance, not only on the earth, but ultimately on all its inhabitants!

As we turn for answers in God's Word, we read the following in Isaiah 14:12–14. "How you are fallen from heaven, O' Lucifer, son of the morning! How you are cut down to the ground, you who weakened the nations! For you have said in your heart, I will ascend into heaven. I will exalt my throne above the stars of God. I will sit on the mount of the congregation. On the farthest sides of the north. I will ascend above the heights of the clouds. I will be like the Most High." God, in turn, replied, "You shall be brought down to Sheol, to the lowest depths of the pit" (Isaiah 14:15). Jesus described the event this way, "I beheld Satan as lightning fall from heaven" (Luke 10:18). Upon his expulsion from heaven to earth along with countless rebellious angels, scholars who adhere to the divine judgment interpretation believe Satan's arrival on earth caused it to become without form and void.

Despite these events, may we be reminded that Almighty God, Elohim, the fullness of deity was totally in charge just as he is today! Please note at this stage while "darkness was on the face of the deep, the Spirit of God was hovering over the face of the waters" (Genesis 1:2). Like a hen taking her chicks under her wings to protect and shield them, the Holy Spirit was, in essence, watching over the earth. From the picture of utter chaos and disaster, Almighty God brought forth an orderly creation.

REBELLION AND UNBELIEF
BRING JUDGMENT

Second Peter 2:4 "God did not spare the angels who
sinned, but cast them down to hell and delivered them
into chains of darkness to be reserved for judgment."

When Satan rebelled in heaven and was cast down to earth,
God told him, "You shall be brought down to Sheol, to the
lowest depths of the pit" (Isaiah 14:15). In studying scripture, we
learn the reason God created hell. It was for the devil and his angels.
Matthew 25:41 says, "Depart from me you cursed into the everlasting fire prepared for the devil and his angels." Personally, I do not
believe God desires one single person to spend eternity in hell. The
Bible says, "The Lord is not slack concerning His promise as some
count slackness, but is longsuffering toward us, not willing that any
should perish but that all should come to repentance" (2 Peter 3:9).
Then we find in Ezekiel 33:11, "As I live, says the Lord God, I have
no pleasure in the death of the wicked, but that the wicked turn from
his way and live."

In the providence of God, Satan, for the time being, is alive
and well. In John 12:31, Jesus said, "Now is the judgment of this
world; now the ruler of this world will be cast out." Jesus called Satan
the "ruler of this world," meaning he has temporary control of this

world's system. You recall in the temptation of Jesus in the wilderness, found in Matthew, chapter 4, Satan offered the world system to Jesus if he would bow down and worship him. The Bible further refers to Satan as the "prince of the power of the air." It seems that Satan's present domain is in the atmospheric heaven, not the third heaven where God dwells; he was expelled from that place. The Bible indicates at times God allows Satan some limited access to his heavenly court, where Satan constantly accuses believers. Job 1:7–8 "The Lord said to Satan, from where do you come?" Satan answered and said, "From going to and fro on the earth and walking back and forth on it."

Hopefully, this gives us insight to what happened in eternity years ago, giving us understanding of the spiritual warfare taking place today. God takes sin, rebellion, and unbelief very seriously. God will and does judge sin! We find a stern warming to all of us in Jude 5 and 6, "I want to remind you, though you once knew this, that the Lord having saved the people out of the land of Egypt, afterward destroyed those who did not believe. And the angels who did not keep their proper domain, but left their own abode, He has reserved in everlasting chains under darkness for the judgment of the Great Day." In the meantime, Satan is busy trying to take as many people with him to hell as possible. "Woe to the inhabitants of the earth and sea! For the Devil has come down to you, having great wrath because he knows his time is short" (Revelation 12:12).

Therefore, we are to "Be sober, be vigilant; because your adversary the Devil walks about like a roaring lion, seeking whom he may devour. Resist him, steadfast in the faith" (1 Peter 5:8–9).

Abundance of Grace

Romans 5:17 "For if by the one man's offense death
reigned through the one, much more those who receive
abundance of grace and of the gift of righteousness
will reign in life through the One, Jesus Christ."

The Bible teaches us a fundamental fact that sin entered the world through one man, Adam. As a result of his sin, death also entered into the world and spread to all men because all of us have sinned and fallen short of the glory of God. On the other hand, God's free gift of grace through the One, our Lord Jesus Christ, abounded to many. While the sin of Adam brought condemnation to all of us, the free gift of grace brought justification.

This gift is for those who are blessed to receive God's abundant and amazing grace. "For by grace you have been saved through faith and that not of yourselves; it is the gift of God, not of works, lest anyone should boast" (Ephesians 2:7–8). Please note in our text this grace is available to those who will receive it! The Bible says, "As many as received Him, to them He gave the right to become children of God, to those who believe in His name; who were born, not of blood, nor of the will of the flesh, nor of the will of man, but of God" (John 1:12–13).

This marvelous gift of grace, I believe, accomplishes far more than we realize. First, it brought us total and complete forgiveness for sins past, present, and future. Not only does God forgive our sin through Christ, but he forgets them! When the enemy attempts to remind us of past sins, which have been confessed and forgiven, appropriate by faith these great promises: "I will forgive their iniquity, and their sin I will remember no more" (Jeremiah 31:34). The psalmist reminds us, "As far as the east is from the west, so far has He removed our transgressions from us" (Psalm 103:12). This is extravagant grace! Remember, our Heavenly Father views us through the soul-cleansing blood of the Lamb. This abundant grace of God also gives us the gift of righteousness. When we receive the Lord Jesus into our hearts by faith, he transfers to our account his righteousness. Hear his Word "being justified freely by His grace through the redemption that is in Christ Jesus, whom God set forth as a propitiation by His blood, through faith, to demonstrate His righteousness ... that He might be just and the Justifier of the one who has faith in Jesus" (Romans 3:24–26). May this marvelous truth sink deep into our hearts and souls. Because of the atoning death of our Lord Jesus on Calvary, we are not only forgiven and cleansed but made righteous and justified freely by his grace. Though we are guilty and hell-deserving sinners, the Judge of all the earth, Almighty God, declares us "not guilty." Jesus took upon himself all of our sin and the penalty of our sin on the cross where he paid the price in full. It was there we were redeemed, bought back from the slavery of sin and death, and set free by the grace and mercy of God.

He Cares For You

First Peter 6 & 7 "Humble yourselves under the mighty hand of God, that He may exalt you in due time, casting all your care upon Him, for he cares for you."

This past week while driving down a major street, I came to a stoplight, which enabled me to read a bumper sticker on the car ahead of me. It read, "Jesus loves you, but I'm His favorite." I was reminded of a very loving former pastor who used to call everyone his favorite. Knowing, in reality, that God is no respecter of persons does not diminish the truth in this context—*you* are his favorite! You are absolutely special to the Lord. I know as I write the Word for the Week today, many are burdened down with care. Please remember our Heavenly Father knows and cares like no one else. He is thinking of you at this very moment. "How precious also are your thoughts to me, O God! How great is the sum of them! If I could count them, they would be more in number than the sand. When I awake, I am still with you" (Psalm 139:17–18).

Are you feeling alone at the moment? You are not, for he has said, "I will never leave you nor forsake you" (Hebrews 13:5). Do you feel the cares you are burdened with are just too much, even for the Lord? They are not! "Call to me, and I will answer you, and show you great and mighty things, which you do not know" (Jeremiah 33:3). "Is there anything too hard for the Lord?" (Genesis 18:14). Of course not!

Our text verse encourages us in humility, to cast all of our care upon the Lord. This involves an act of faith and trust on our part. Because of our human frailty, we often make the effort to cast our care on the Lord, but then we pick it right back up. Our self-dependency sometimes makes it extremely difficult for us to let go and let God do what we cannot do. His is the mighty hand, the unfailing hand, which will always triumph on our behalf. "Cast your burden on the Lord, and He will sustain you; He shall never permit the righteous to be moved" (Psalm 55:22).

When I was a boy, there was an old hymn (we never sing anymore) that comes to mind. It was entitled, "Leave It There." The lyrics are very appropriate, "Leave it there, leave it there, take your burden to the Lord and leave it there. If you trust and never doubt, He will surely bring you out, take your burden to the Lord and leave it there." Is this not a great truth in line with the promise in our text, "He may exalt you in due time."

"Call upon me in the day of trouble; I will deliver you, and you shall glorify me," (Psalm 50:15). He will deliver you from care, heartache, or any trouble. In the process, you will glorify him! To God be the glory, great things he has done.

The City of the King

Psalm 122:6 "Pray for the peace of Jerusalem;
may they prosper who love you."

Tucked away in this psalm is a most interesting request, or perhaps command. We are encouraged to pray for the peace of Jerusalem and at the same time, a prayer for prosperity is desired for all who love her. Jerusalem has and always will be of great biblical significance. The Bible refers to it often. "There is a river whose streams shall make glad the City of God" (Psalm 46:4). "Great is the Lord, and greatly to be praised in the City of God, in His holy mountain. Beautiful in elevation. The joy of the whole earth, is Mount Zion on the sides of the North. The city of the Great King... God will establish it forever" (Psalm 48:1–2, 8b).

We know from biblical history that God chose the Jewish people, the Israelites, to be the recipients of the law, the covenants, the promises, the service of God and through the seed of Abraham, our Lord and Savior Jesus Christ. It was God's intention that Israel be committed to him and ultimately would lead others, including the Gentiles, to believe in Jehovah God. The Lord also gave to Israel the land of Canaan. "I give to you and your descendants after you the land in which you are a stranger, all the land of Canaan, as an everlasting possession," (Genesis 17:8).

Although Israel has not fulfilled the divine plan of God and is temporarily set aside until the fullness of the Gentiles has come, be sure that Almighty God will keep his covenant with Israel and will yet fulfill every promise he made to Abraham. "Now the Lord had said to Abram; Get thee out of your country, from your family and from your father's house to a land that I will show you. I will make you a great nation; I will bless you and make your name great; and you shall be a blessing. I will bless those who bless you, and I will curse him who curses you; and in you all the families of the earth shall be blessed" (Genesis 12:1–3).

One of the reasons God has prospered America is because as a nation, we have stood by Israel as her strongest ally and friend. I pray we will continue to do so until Jesus comes, for there are many who would desire Israel to give up land, which God gave them years ago through the Patriarch Abraham, not to mention those who desire her total destruction. Israel has been despised by some for many years, just as many hate her today. Psalm 83:1–4 is just as true today as it was hundreds of years ago. "Do not keep silent, O God! Do not hold thy peace. And do not be still, O God! For behold, your enemies make a tumult; and those who hate you have lifted up their head. They have taken crafty counsel together against your sheltered ones. They have said, "Come and let us cut them off from being a nation, that the name of Israel may be remembered no more." Is this not the wicked desire of the Iranian president, Ahmadinejad? He would like nothing better, as well as Hamas, Hezbollah, and Syria. We know with certainty God will never allow this to happen.

Pray for the peace of Jerusalem, for Israel, and especially for revival in America.

A Great Asset

Proverbs 22:1 "A good name is rather to be chosen than great riches and loving favor rather than silver and gold."

What is in a name? Quite a lot, to be exact. In our secular society, name recognition can be very lucrative. Think of the millions of dollars sports figures and celebrities make on endorsements, simply by allowing their names to be used in conjunction with a certain product. While most of us are not influenced to buy a product because of an endorsement, we do sometimes purchase name-brand items from motor vehicles to electronics because they carry a "trusted" name.

It is not only possible, but more likely probable, that many who attain wealth from endorsements do not have the kind of "good name" the scripture references. What do you imagine when you think of someone having a good name? Is it not such things as honesty, diligent and hard-working, dependable, trustworthy, faithful, etc.? A person who loves God, their family, and country?

My dad was a poor man, a painter by trade. When he went home to be with the Lord, very unexpectedly at the age of sixty-one, he did not leave his children anything of monetary value. He had just enough life insurance, which allowed us to give him a respectable funeral, but my dad left his children something far greater than riches. He left us his "good name." Although I do not remember my dad saying, "I love you, son," it was always understood and never questioned that he loved me. His actions and his lifestyle spoke much louder than any words he could say. He was a loving man who loved everyone and was loved likewise by all who knew him. My dad had a good name!

As I write this today, I am reminded of the many in the Bible with good names. Abraham, a friend of God. David, a man after God's own heart. Jeremiah, the weeping prophet. Paul, the beloved servant of God. Mary, the young maid chosen to give birth to God's precious son. Lazarus, a dear friend of Jesus. Esther, faithful unto death. Joshua and Caleb, totally committed to God. Mary, who anointed Jesus with the costly oil in preparation for his death on Calvary. All of these and many more with good names. What kind of name will you and I leave for those who come behind us, even our children.

What's in a name? When the angel of the Lord appeared to Joseph, who was engaged to Mary, after explaining that her conception was of the Holy Spirit, he said, "She shall bring forth a son, and thou shall call His name Jesus; for He shall save His people from their sins" (Matthew 1:21).

"Neither is there salvation in any other; for there is no other name under heaven given among men, whereby we must be saved" (Acts 4:12). The world can laugh and reject the precious name of Jesus as Savior and Lord, but God will have the last word.

"Wherefore, God also has highly exalted him and given him a name which is above every name, that at the name of Jesus, every knee should bow and every tongue should confess that Jesus Christ is Lord, to the glory of God, the Father" (Philippians 2:9 –11).

Agony in the Garden

Matthew 26:36 — "Then cometh Jesus with them into a place called Gethsemane and says unto the disciples, sit here, while I go and pray yonder. And he took with him Peter and the two sons of Zebedee and began to be sorrowful and very depressed."

How seldom, if ever, do we read the message of Gethsemane and realize even in part what our Lord endured. The anticipation of the cross, with all it involved, weighed heavy on his spirit, his heart, his very being! Being both God and man, yet without sin, his burden was enormous. He was sorrowful as the Son of God, his spiritual being, and as the Son of man.

Most all of us have experienced times of tremendous burdens, which sometimes can lead to a state of depression such as our Lord experienced. What do we do in such times as these? At first, it may cause us to withdraw from everyone, but then as we work through it, we cry out to God for help. Usually, our next step is to contact family and friends to solicit their prayers. This is what Jesus did. As he went into the Garden under the weight of the cross to speak with his Heavenly Father, he brought along his close associates, the disciples, and ask that they pray with him and for him. Going farther into the Garden, he brought only his closest friends, Peter, James, and John, to intercede for him. Can you imagine that he would eventually "ever live to make intercession for us" and was now himself desperately in need of intercession. We fail to realize that he "was in all points tempted like as we are, yet without sin" (Hebrews 4:15b). Our great High Priest is touched with the feeling of our infinities. May our troubled hearts find consolation in the knowledge that he walked before us through all of life's difficulties and will walk with us through our difficulties.

Although in need of prayer support there in the Garden, he found none! Several times he urges his friends to watch with him and pray, but to no avail. Upon seeking them, the Bible says, "He came and found them asleep again, for their eyes were heavy" (Matthew 26:43). In their defense, Jesus said, "The spirit indeed is willing, but the flesh is weak." I am quite certain any of us would have failed him as they did.

Going into the Garden with Peter, James, and John, it becomes apparent, from scripture, the agony of his soul. At this point, he tells them, "My soul is exceedingly sorrowful, even unto death." He is now alone with our Heavenly Father. As he looks into the bitter cup he will be drinking, he cries out, "O my Father, if it be possible let this cup pass from me; nevertheless, not as I will but as thou wilt" (Matthew 26:39). Two more times he prays similar words, "O my Father, if this cup may not pass away from me except I drink it, thy will be done" (Matthew 26:42).

The Good Shepherd

John 12:27 "Now is my soul troubled; and what shall I say? Father, save me from this hour; but for this cause came I unto this hour."

As the anticipation of all that was to come upon him, looking into the cup he chose to drink, the Lord's sweat turned to great drops of blood. He had predicted his death to his disciples. "Behold we go up to Jerusalem; and the Son of Man shall be betrayed unto the Chief Priests and Scribes, and they shall condemn Him to death and shall deliver Him to the Gentiles to mock and to scourge and to crucify Him. And the third day He shall rise again" (Matthew 20:18–19). The weight of the cross and the price he must pay to redeem us was almost more than even our Lord could bear. Humanly speaking, he could have died there in the Garden from loss of blood, but that was not God's divine plan. He was destined to die outside the gate on Mt. Calvary as the Lamb of God who takes away the sin of the world. He was a lamb slain before the foundation of the world; the fulfillment of many precious promises of God, beginning with Genesis 3:15.

Nevertheless, we find it is necessary for the Heavenly Father to intervene there in the Garden as our Savior agonizes. For the Bible says, "And there appeared an angel unto Him from Heaven, strengthening Him" (Luke 22:43). When we really get the full meaning of this scene in Gethsemane, identifying as much as is humanly possible with our Lord, it is as though, like Moses, we can hear Almighty God saying, "Put off thy shoes from off thy feet, for the place whereon you stand is Holy ground."

It is nothing less than incredible that God could love us so much than to send his precious son, himself a willing sacrifice to make atonement for all who would come to him in repentance of sin and faith in his finished work. Andrew Murray says it well, "In God, love reaches its highest point and is the culmination of His glory. In the man Christ Jesus on the cross, love is at its highest. We owe everything to this love. Love is the power that moved Christ to die for us. In love, God highly exalted Him as Lord and Savior."

As we study the Gospels, we find from the very first time he begins to prepare his disciples for his death and resurrection (Matthew 16:21), through his earthly ministry, Jesus never for a moment turns from his commitment. Faithful unto death! As we observe him praying in the Garden, even though he asks if it may be possible for the cup to pass from him, he always concludes by saying, "Nevertheless, not my will but thine be done" (Luke 22:42b). Not a wonder Paul wrote, "I beseech you therefore brethren, by the mercies of God, that you present your bodies a living sacrifice, holy acceptable unto God, which is your reasonable service" (Romans 12:1).

Consider the Cup

Luke 22:42 "Father, if thou be willing, remove this cup from me; nevertheless, not my will, but thine be done."

Come with me in your mind's eye, in your heart of hearts, to the Garden of Gethsemane. See our Savior praying alone to our Heavenly Father. He is in agony, sorrowful and depressed as he looks into the bitter cup he is soon to drink. As we put the Gospels together, we find that several times he has asked the Father to remove this dreaded cup; to let it pass from him. Even while asking, however, our Lord knew if he did not drink the cup, all of us would die in our sins, banished from the presence of God for eternity in a hell of fire prepared for the devil and his angels.

What did Jesus see in the cup? While it is impossible for us to know, we can be sure of several things. Jesus, the holy, sinless Son of God would not only die for our sin, but would literally be made sin for us. "For he has made him, who knew no sin, to be sin for us, that we might be made the righteousness of God in him" (2 Corinthians 5:21). We cannot imagine the horror to his holy being. Every filthy sin ever committed by depraved man from creation to the end of time would be placed upon the sinless Son of God. No wonder he was sorrowful and very depressed.

Then Jesus knew that on Calvary's cross, as he made complete atonement for our sin, the full fury of the wrath of God that rightly should fall upon us would fall upon him. The Bible says, "It pleased the Lord to bruise him; he has put him to grief. When thou shall make his soul an offering for sin ... He shall see of the travail of His soul, and shall be satisfied; by his knowledge shall my righteous servant justify many; for he shall bear their iniquities" (Isaiah 53:10–11). "Surely he has borne our grief and carried our sorrow, yet we did esteem him stricken, smitten of God and afflicted" (Isaiah 53:4). Looking into the cup, the Lord Jesus saw not only would he become sin for us but also would pay the penalty for our sin.

Try to understand, this was enormous torment for our Lord to endure. As the sinless and only Son of Almighty God, he, unlike us, was always completely in the perfect will of God. Hear his own words, "I have kept my Father's commandments and abide in his love. When you have lifted up the Son of man, then shall you know that I am he, and that I do nothing of myself; but as my Father has taught me, I speak these things" (John's Gospel).

As if these two things were not enough, I believe more than anything, Jesus drew back at the very thought of his Heavenly Father having to turn his back on him as he died alone on Calvary. As he would make his soul an offering for our sin, would become sin for us, God would have to turn from his beloved Son for a time. Jesus, for a time, would have to be forsaken, or cut off from the Father as we should all be. Thus, we hear him cry from the cross, "My God, my God, why have you forsaken me?" (Matthew 27:46).

Not a wonder then, when praying in the Garden, we find these words, "And being in agony, he prayed more earnestly; and his sweat was, as it were, great drops of blood falling down to the ground" (Luke 22:44).

A Sinless Life

Romans 3:24–26 "Being justified freely by his grace through the redemption that is in Christ Jesus, whom God has set forth to be a propitiation through faith in his blood, to declare his righteousness for the remission of sins that are past, through the forbearance of God; to declare, I say at this time his righteousness, that he might be just and the justifier of him who believes in Jesus."

It was essential that the Lord Jesus Christ be virgin-born for had he merely been a good man of human birth, he could never have been our Redeemer. He was rather the God-Man, 100 percent God and 100 percent man, yet without sin. Since he was and is the divine, sinless Son of Almighty God, he did not have the sinful nature all of us inherited from Adam. Consequently, since he never committed a single sin, the law of God had no claim upon him. He is totally righteous and holy. "The Lord is righteous in all his ways and holy in all his works" (Psalm 145:17).

Since he alone was just in the way he lived, he is able to satisfy through his atoning death all the demands of God's law. His was an exclusive life, our Great High Priest after the order of Melchizedek. The Bible says, "For we have not an high priest who cannot be touched with the feeling of our infirmities, but was in all points tempted like as we are, yet without sin" (Hebrews 4:15). The saving life of Christ, coupled with his atoning dearth, enables us to become righteous in him. For Isaiah well described us before we were born again. "But we are all as an unclean thing and our righteousnesses are as filthy rags" (Isaiah 64:6). Aside from the saving grace of the Lord, none of us could ever become righteous. "Who can say, I have made my heart clean, I am pure from my sin" (Proverbs 20:9).

The sacrificial death of the Lord Jesus on Calvary's cross enables us to be clothed in his righteousness so that we who are guilty of sin and condemnation are now considered justified through faith in him. "For He has made Him, who knew no sin, to be sin for us, that we might be made the righteousness of God in Him" (2 Corinthians 5:21).

"God commended His love toward us in that, while we were yet sinners, Christ died for us. Much more then, being now justified by His blood, we shall be saved from wrath through Him. For if, when we were enemies we were reconciled to God by the death of His Son, much more, being reconciled, we shall be saved by His life" (Romans 5:8–10).

Precious Redeemer

1 Peter 1:18–20 "For as much as you know that you were not redeemed with corruptible things, like silver and gold, from your vain manner of life received by tradition from your fathers, but with the precious blood of Christ, as of a lamb without blemish and without spot, who verily was foreordained before the foundation of the world, but was manifest in these last times for you."

As we further consider our Blessed Redeemer, I feel most inadequate to even try to expound on his majesty, power, love, and grace. As John the Beloved Disciple wrote in the Gospel of John when he said if all that should be written about Jesus were written, the world could not contain the books. There are several things I do want us to consider, however.

Because of his eternal foreknowledge, God knew that man, originally formed for the purpose of fellowshipping with him, would fall into sin and thus lose his relationship with him. The Heavenly Father also knew unless he personally intervened, all of mankind would forever be without hope. Man would live and die physically then be banished into an eternal hell of fire prepared for the devil and his angels.

As we consider not only our own sinfulness but the multiplied sin of the world, we could quite easily ask, why should God care what happens to us? We would all be getting what we justly deserved. Yet despite our sin, John 3:16 clearly indicates it is in fact the great love of God that causes him to care. This love is immeasurable, indescribable, and totally undeserved. Yet he still loves us. My finite mind can find no other explanation but *grace!*

Consider now for all eternity the Triune God, Father, Son, and Holy Spirit are One. One before the world was ever created, One in creation, One throughout the history of mankind to this present day, and will throughout eternity still be One. First John 5:7 "For there are three that bear record in Heaven, the Father, The Word, and the Holy Spirit; and these three are one." In light of this truth, we can believe then that just as the three were One in creation, they were One in agreement that God the Father, because of his love for lost mankind, would be willing to give his only Son as a willing sacrifice to redeem man from sin and its penalty. This agreement was made before the world was ever formed, thus the Lord Jesus is "the Lamb slain before the foundation of the world." A perfect and willing sacrifice without spot or blemish.

Consider how blessed we are that he has been made manifest to us in these last days. John describes it this way, "And the Word was made flesh and dwelt among us [and we beheld his glory, the glory as of the only begotten of the Father] full of grace and truth" (John 1:14). The disciples experienced firsthand the Lord Jesus, having walked with him and served him for about three and one-half years. Some, like Peter, James and John, saw him transfigured before them on the mountain. "His face did shine like the sun and His raiment was as white as the light" (Matthew 17:2). These literally beheld his glory.

While only a few participated in this glorious occasion, we who know him as Savior and Lord, are still blessed because through his Holy Spirit, he has revealed himself to us as our Redeemer. Jesus said, "All things are delivered unto me by my Father and no man knoweth the Son, but the Father; neither knoweth any man the Father, except the Son, and he to whomsoever the Son will reveal him" (Matthew 11:27).

The Holy City of the Future

Hebrews 11:8–10 "By faith Abraham obeyed when called to go out to the place which he would receive as an inheritance. And he went out, not knowing where he was going. By faith he dwelt in the land of promise as in a foreign country, dwelling in tents with Isaac and Jacob, the heirs with him of the same promise; for he waited for the city which has foundations whose builder and maker is God."

This passage reminds me of the song, "This World is Not My Home." Abraham, though in the land of promise, considered himself in a foreign country. He looked beyond the here and now by faith for his heavenly home. I do not know about you, but like Abraham, I feel very much as though I were living in a foreign country. America as we once knew it is no more. Almost daily our liberties and freedoms are being taken away as we rapidly move toward a socialist society. Personally, I believe we, the people of God, are paying for our sins. Like Israel of old, we have forsaken the God of our youth, Jehovah God, to enjoy the pleasures of sin for a season.

When we, through faith in Christ, repent of our sin and return to the Lord, we will find as Abraham did that we too will be looking forward to the City of God and the New Jerusalem. Are we not all tired of the sin in our society? Do we not long in our spirit for a better place? The Bible tells us that even creation looks forward to our complete redemption, for it will be delivered from the bondage of corruption, the effect of man's sin, resulting in death and decay. "The creation itself also will be delivered from the bondage of corruption into the glorious liberty of the children of God. For we know that the whole creation groans and labors with birth pangs together until now" (Romans 8:21–22).

Thank the Lord in Christ our future is very bright! When the Lord begins to reign during the millennium, the Bible says, "They shall not hurt nor destroy in all my holy mountain. For the earth shall be full of the knowledge of the Lord as the waters cover the sea" (Isaiah 11:9). The Lord will reign from his beloved city of Jerusalem, as Israel will be restored during the Kingdom Age. "Thus says the Lord: I will return to Zion and dwell in the midst of Jerusalem. Jerusalem shall be called the City of Truth, the mountain of the Lord of Hosts, the Holy Mountain" (Zechariah 8:3). Quite unlike Washington, DC.

Until that great day, may the Lord help each of us to be sanctified for him. Then, like faithful Abraham, we too can look forward to our new heavenly home prepared for those who know and love him. Where "eye has not seen, nor ear heard, nor have entered into the heart of man the things which God has prepared for those who love Him" (1 Corinthians 2:9). In the meantime, may our Heavenly Father help each of us to stay focused on him, pray for the peace of Jerusalem, for America, and for one another.

About the Author

Walt was born and raised in New Orleans, Louisiana, and immediately upon graduating from high school, he joined the Navy. After completing Basic Training, Walt was stationed in Jacksonville, Florida, at NAS. It was there the Lord spoke to his heart, convicting him of his need for a personal relationship with God; and through divine intervention, the Lord used a pastor in New Orleans to lead him to faith in Christ by way of a long-distance call. Walt's life was greatly transformed by the power of the Gospel.

An insurance agent/broker since his twenty-first birthday, Walt became a student of God's Word and began teaching the Bible, and he has done this now for over fifty years.

Believing in the divine inspiration of scripture, its miraculous preservation, and its life-changing power, Walt had the desire to publish a devotional book, but with work and family, he did not seem to have the time. One day, the Lord laid on his heart to write one devotion a week, which he began approximately ten years ago. He named it, "Word for the Week" and e-mailed it to family and friends. The publication of this book is the fulfillment of a dream come true for Walt and wife, Kathy. Their prayer is that this book will be used to encourage and build up the Body of Christ.

Walt lives with his wife, Kathy, in Denton, Texas. They have two sons, one daughter, six grandsons, one granddaughter, and five great-grandchildren.

CPSIA information can be obtained
at www.ICGtesting.com
Printed in the USA
FSOW01n0107120717
36047FS